THE INSIDE STORY
OF BRITAIN'S MOST NOTORIOUS HEIST

HATTON
GARDEN

THE INSIDE STORY
OF BRITAIN'S MOST NOTORIOUS HEIST

HATTON GARDEN

JONATHAN LEVI
WITH EMMA FRENCH

BLINK
bringing you closer

Published by Blink Publishing
3.08, The Plaza,
535 Kings Road,
Chelsea Harbour,
London, SW10 0SZ

www.blinkpublishing.co.uk

facebook.com/blinkpublishing
twitter.com/blinkpublishing

Paperback – 978-1-911600-42-8
eBook – 978-1-911600-56-5

A CIP catalogue of this book is available from the British Library.

Designed by Envy Design
Printed and bound by Clays Ltd, St. Ives Plc

3 5 7 9 10 8 6 4 2

Blink Publishing is an imprint of the Bonnier Publishing Group
www.bonnierpublishing.co.uk

This book is dedicated to everyone in the gutter
who dared to look up at the stars

CONTENTS

AUTHOR'S NOTE   1

PROLOGUE: **BREAKING INTO THE BUBBLE**   5

CHAPTER ONE: **SETTING THE SCENE**   7

CHAPTER TWO: **GETTING ACQUAINTED**   15

CHAPTER THREE: **NUTS AND BOLTS**   33

CHAPTER FOUR: **AND SO IT BEGINS**   57

CHAPTER FIVE: **PROBLEMS**   95

CHAPTER SIX: **THE BIG WIN**   119

CHAPTER SEVEN: **THE ESCAPE**   127

CHAPTER EIGHT: **THE DISCOVERY**   141

CHAPTER NINE: **THE LOOT**   155

CHAPTER TEN: **THE SURVEILLANCE** 183

CHAPTER ELEVEN: **THE ARREST** 215

CHAPTER TWELVE: **THE CASE** 231

CHAPTER THIRTEEN: **THE PRISON** 251

CHAPTER FOURTEEN: **MORE DRAMA** 265

CHAPTER FIFTEEN: **WHERE'S BASIL?** 271

EPILOGUE 287

AUTHOR'S NOTE

I am Jonathan Levi and this is the story of my investigation into the men behind the Hatton Garden heist, from the robbery's inception to Belmarsh and beyond. I am an executive producer in television, mostly in documentaries. In a nutshell, that means that I get paid to originate, pitch and execute ideas for new TV shows. Part of my sell is my ability to get access to hard-to-reach people or places, gain trust, format the show, sell it to a network and deliver it, ideally in the same way I sold it in the first place.

This work is based on a year of extensive research both for this book and for a small role I've had on a prime-time ITV drama series. I have included never-before-published transcripts of covert police recordings, I have had direct contact with the robbers in Belmarsh as well as access to their friends and close family members who would act as messengers between us and the gang. I have spoken off the record to senior police officers and members of the judiciary who were closest to the case; and as much as possible, and most importantly, all the way through the book we have stuck to the gang's own words and tried to tell this unfolding story in their own words. Every effort has been made to stick faithfully to the facts. The objective is for the sum total of all this work to be an engaging and accurate portrait into the greatest robbery of our generation.

It is important to emphasise that no money has exchanged hands and, although this book is based largely on first-hand testimony and exciting revelations, I am not in any way the mouthpiece of, or complicit with, the Hatton Garden robbers.

My initial interest in the Hatton Garden robbers came out of another story entirely. It dates back as far as 2012 when, through my underworld contacts, I had been trying to produce a documentary about London's most famous crime family, The Adams

AUTHOR'S NOTE

Family. I wanted to tell the early story of this big Roman Catholic family growing up in Islington, how they got into crime, and follow their story up until the famous shoot-out against the Reillys, a rival gang.

I circled the Adams family and got to know people close to them. Just as I was making some real progress, the Hatton Garden robbery went down over that fateful Easter weekend in 2015. Suddenly I had a big crime story to jump on and I already knew some of the people involved. An exciting, real-life story. And as luck would have it, it was a story that the press jumped on and everyone was talking about.

It was by no means a victimless crime, but if you didn't lose anything yourself that day it could just about look that way. No one got hurt, no one was tied up, no one got doused in petrol and threatened. It seemed ingenious, with an almost Robin Hood-like quality to it. Half-inching gold bars and diamonds from the rich, where the booty was probably nicked already, being hidden for some nefarious purpose or already insured – it captured the imagination. What a story: an elderly gang working together, finding treasure and running off into the sunset.

One of the hardest things about a book like this is ferreting out the real story, the untold story. Ignoring the noise and the hype, editing out all the speculation and hearsay and only listening to those people who actually lived and breathed it. From both sides. From the point of view of the gang, the families and friends of the gang and also of the police and judiciary. The people that really know what happened, who did what, who said what, whose job it really was and how it all unravelled after the event. I have made the deliberate decision to collate all this information from all my criminal and police sources, but not to reveal exactly who said what and what came from whom.

This is mostly to protect myself and my family. But it is something I made clear to everyone involved when they talked to me so they could speak freely, without worrying about the consequences. I talked to gang members and also members of their wider social circle. At times I felt jumpy. At times excited. And each time I spoke to someone I went home and told my wife, a writer, and we started, painstakingly, to capture this intriguing story in written form. This book is the accumulation of all those conversations, and we wrote it together over many evenings, late nights and weekends. I believe it is the most accurate and truthful telling of the biggest robbery of our time. It has been a pleasure and a privilege to go on this journey.

PROLOGUE:
BREAKING INTO THE BUBBLE

Terry held his breath as his old friend Danny and their accomplice Basil began to work the pump that powered the hydraulic ram. The tense hours, days, months and years had all been leading up to this point. They'd got through the wall, but that was only stage one. Stage two was toppling the heavy metal cabinet that stood between them and untold riches.

Danny pumped frantically until the prop was braced tightly against the wall and the jack. Terry had tried to help, but the strain on him was obvious to the other two men, who had motioned for him to stop.

They had failed at this once before. Their accomplices,

Brian and Carl, had walked away after the previous pump broke, leaving Terry, Danny and Basil to give it a final go two nights later.

As Danny pumped again, there was a loud crack.

'Fucking hell Danny,' Terry wheezed. 'Careful. That goes again, we're fucked.'

Danny gritted his teeth and kept at it. More pumping. Loud hissing. Then a huge bang.

Danny winced at the noise, massaging his eyelids with his index fingers to try to take the pain away. He blinked his eyes open again as the dust settled. They were no longer faced with a dull metal cabinet. The promised land lay before them.

Processing the gang's implausible success against the odds, Danny's thoughts then turned to his disbelief that Brian and Carl had walked away.

'Never give it a chance, Tel, did they?

The three men peered together into the hole. Beyond it, 999 treasure-filled safe deposit boxes.

'We've fucking done it!' the three robbers said at once.

CHAPTER ONE
SETTING THE SCENE

Hatton Garden is both a street and an area in the London Borough of Camden. It has been London's jewellery quarter since at least medieval times, and it is the centre of the British diamond trade. For many years it was undeniably the global centre of the jewellery trade, and it retains huge importance. It has housed, and continues to house, some of the world's biggest brands in precious metal and gems.

The name 'Hatton Garden' itself is an ancient one, coming from the garden of Ely Place, the London residence of the Bishop of Ely. Ely Place was gifted to Sir Christopher Hatton by Elizabeth I in 1581, during a vacancy of the see. He was one of her favourite courtiers, handsome and a good dancer, and Elizabeth evidently viewed Hatton Garden as a suitable prize for him.

There are almost 300 jewellery businesses in Hatton Garden today as well as over 55 jewellery shops, more than anywhere else in Britain. Legendary international diamond brand De Beers has a huge headquarters right behind the main shopping concourse of Hatton Garden. Another notable store opening took place in 1962, when Laurence Graff of the Wittelsbach-Graff Diamond dynasty opened up. Get a room of women together and the chances are that some of them will be wearing engagement rings chosen for them in Hatton Garden... including my own wife.

Plenty of Hatton Garden's action takes place underground too, in both senses. Below the pavement are office spaces, workshops, tunnels and, of course, vaults. Hatton Garden lies on the western edge of the City, London's financial hub. It is also in close proximity to some of London's leading law establishments, but the legality of what takes place in the Garden is sometimes far more questionable.

Today the place has an edge. Although bustling and traffic-clogged on weekdays, on a Sunday or Bank

Holiday morning, the place has an eerie feel. On these days it's virtually empty but there is a slightly paranoid, twitchy atmosphere to the place. There are invariably odd characters skulking around, glancing down the street, at their mobile phones and back again. It is a street that is at once quintessentially London and also entirely foreign.

Architecturally it is a strange mishmash of crumbling period properties and modern office blocks. Rather like Amsterdam's diamond district, the extraordinary riches laid out in the reinforced shop windows are strangely at odds with the seedy atmosphere and middle-aged male proprietors glancing up cautiously from display cases, always scanning up and down the street.

I have walked down to Hatton Garden from my office during the lunch hour and after work many, many times. On one particular Wednesday in May 2017, almost exactly two years after the heist, the atmosphere was even more charged than usual. I stood opposite 88–90 and those now-famous double black doors listening to the conversations around me. The left of the two black doors to the Hatton Garden Safety Deposit LTD was open and a steady stream of people went in and out. Security guards eyed me up from the various shops. Jewellers hurried by. I looked up at the white CCTV camera on Greville Street.

More than living up to its shady reputation, in the space of a few minutes, snippets of conversation included: 'They went about blabbing all over London. If they had just kept their mouths shut they would have got away with it.' I resisted the temptation to interrupt these strangers' conversations with my own insights and walked off down Greville Street.

The area is full of secret places and mysterious buildings. The monks of Ely had dug tunnels around the Garden and the River Fleet was channelled into a network of underground waterways. Inside these buildings were once warrens of small rooms, rented out to jewellery makers with diverse skillsets. Metal doors and multiple locks protected the specialist jewellery craftsmen – but they also helped leading figures in London's underworld keep away from the prying eyes of the law.

A trawl through old newspaper cuttings reveals many robberies took place in Hatton Garden shops or upon commuting traders, including the murder of Hatton Garden diamond merchant Leo Grunhut who was shot outside his Golders Green home in 1978 while carrying £250,000 in diamonds. The area was a particular target for burglars and safeblowers – in a three-month period during 1987 Hatton Garden suffered six robberies and ten burglaries. In July 1993 thieves stole £7 million worth of gems belonging to the jewellers Graff Diamonds. At the time it was London's biggest gem heist but it was, of course, trumped by the 2015 Hatton Garden job – the latest and greatest in this tempting zone of Aladdin's Cave riches.

News of the robbery first broke after the police made it public, on 7 April 2015. The BBC simply reported 'Hatton Garden Safety Deposit Box Vault Burgled' and laid out the very basic facts that were known at that point:

'Burglars have used heavy cutting equipment to break into safety deposit boxes in a vault in London's jewellery quarter. The raid is thought to have happened over the Easter bank holiday weekend at the Hatton Garden Safe Deposit company. BBC News correspondent Ben Ando, who is at the scene, said: "What is not clear at the moment is when the thieves actually broke in or how they broke in. Diamond jewellery expert Lewis Malka, who works in the area, said the haul was likely to amount to "hundreds and hundreds of thousands of pounds".'

Soon after the robbery took place, I asked my

underworld contact who the guys were and he just smiled. He claimed not to know anything. But when their names were published in the press after they had been arrested, I wrote him a letter and he promised he could get to them. I started looking into the robbery, really looking into it, reading every article that had been published, and I tried to track down people in north London that actually knew these people. I gained access to all of the police transcripts and pored over them in great detail.

What struck me, that I had not seen anywhere else, was that the unobtrusive and eccentric Danny Jones – famous for not being famous, and known by every firm and villain in town but never in the limelight – seemed like he might genuinely be at the centre of the job. His half-smile in the mugshot, the mischief in his eyes. I suspected that Danny knew more about this robbery than anyone else. And everyone else seemed to have largely ignored him. This felt significant.

At this stage, I put my TV hat on, asked around and had a think about how to approach the story. A Sky Atlantic series? An ITV1 drama? How many episodes? My head was spinning.

Something that was driven home in every subsequent interaction I had with the gang was that this was the story of old-fashioned criminals. They were a dying breed, committing a very British crime. The Hatton Garden robbery was the last big job not just for the four ringleaders but for their entire generation of London underworld figures. The infamous "North London gangster belt" of Enfield, Barnet and Cockfosters drew the attention of police surveillance in a way it was hard to believe that big future crime stories would. The settings have changed. Crime has changed. But not for these guys…

CHAPTER TWO

GETTING ACQUAINTED

'It's fucking working 'cos you're egging one another on.' (Terry Perkins)

I already had a strong relationship with a figure in the underworld who I am going to call 'Arthur'. I am being as open in this story as I can possibly be, but you don't need to know for the purposes of this story, and I need to keep my skull intact. Arthur certainly helped me significantly along the way, both by granting access to the gang and by elucidating many aspects of the north London crime scene to me, and I am eternally grateful to him.

The story was taking me over a little bit, maybe because I was tantalisingly close to getting to know the robbers. Perhaps it was because I'd been hanging out in a bunch of the same north London places that they did and with quite a few of the same people.

There weren't many letters I'd written in my life into which I put as much thought as the one to Danny Jones. I prepared a letter to send to him at Belmarsh with an identical one to go to Val Jones, his common-law wife.

Dear Danny,

My name is Jonathan Levi and I am a friend of [Arthur]. [Arthur]'s pal *** has hopefully sent you a letter about me.

I work for a major television production company in London. We produce television programmes and films for all the major television channels in the UK – ITV, the BBC and Channel 4 – and around the world.

For instance I made two films about Broadmoor – it was the first time anybody has ever filmed on the inside and I had full access to the all the patients and staff. It took me five years to get the access and a year to make it.

I also made a film with the X Factor judge Tulisa about her drug entrapment with The Sun on Sunday. I told the story from Tulisa's perspective over the course of a year. She trusted me and let me into her world, and as a result I was able to tell her story and our film changed the way people thought about her and her case.

If you agree, I would like to tell your story about Hatton Garden – and to tell it as much as possible in your words – what happened, how it happened and how you feel about it all. Both the BBC and Film4 have told me they are very interested in a film about Hatton Garden. It is after all the biggest and most audacious robbery in history!

I appreciate that visits are tight. But if it would be possible to invite me for one visit I'd be really grateful. In the meantime if you agree, could I write a list of questions and give them to your wife to give to you? And she could relay your answers back to us? I would like to find a way to work together to tell your story so let me know what you think, what questions immediately come to mind and how you would like to proceed.

Yours sincerely,

Jonathan Levi

Then all I could do was wait.

My day job certainly takes me to all kinds of diverse and fascinating places. When the call came, I was in London Transgender Surgery on Wimpole Street W1. My phone rang and it was a guy called Jon on the line, who would become a very important player in this drama. For now, though, he was just introducing himself as the representative of Danny Jones and Terry Perkins.

'They want to talk.'

I stepped out of the clinic and walked round to the corner of Harley Street. Excitement. The letter had worked. They would talk to me.

Wherever I had been expecting the first meeting to take place, it wasn't a pub next to a garden centre on Cattlegate Road in Enfield. I drove though Hadley Wood in Cockfosters and out onto long, empty country roads. It is beautiful in that rural part of Enfield. I'd grown up in south-west London and gone to school in Hammersmith in the 1990s, and my acquaintance with the north London gangster belt was all new.

The road narrowed and I slowed down for a speed camera and drove past several large garden centres. I was on the right road. It said Crews Hill on my satnav and the pub we were meeting at was coming up in 100 yards. As instructed by Jon, who had called the meeting, I pulled in and parked next to a top-of-the-range white Range Rover with blacked-out windows. I felt a little nervous as I pushed open the pub door and stepped inside.

Jon and Val, Danny's common-law wife, were standing together by the bar. They both turned and smiled and Jon put his hand out for a shake. I kissed Val on the cheek and offered them both a drink. Jon asked for a beer, so I joined him. It was the end of summer and still warm outside, and that meant more potential eavesdroppers about than we had anticipated. We went outside and sat at a wooden table a little way from any of the others.

I studied Val. Maybe forties? Slim, brunette and nicely but conservatively dressed. She was in one sense the classic glamorous gangster's moll, with a glint in her eye. Warm, good-humoured and less guarded than I had expected, I sensed from the beginning she and I could work together. Jon was going to be a tougher nut to crack. He sported gold bracelets, a large Rolex and a thick gold necklace. He was in blue jeans and a T-shirt and seemed more jumpy than Val.

'So,' he started, I am close family with Danny, and

Val is a very private person so she wants me here. And, I've been told that if we talk to anyone we ought to talk to you. That we can trust you and that you made that documentary with Tulisa and also that one inside Broadmoor. I liked that Broadmoor one. What's Tulisa like then?'

'Tulisa went to hell and back,' I said, 'and I followed what she went through and tried to tell her story as truthfully and as accurately as I could. She was massively misunderstood and completely innocent...'

'I've looked you up,' said Val. 'You've done some good stuff. You have to understand that I have been very paranoid about all this. Not talking to no one and keeping myself to myself.'

'I understand,' I said. It must have been a hell of a lot of pressure going through the court case and seeing Danny on the front page of all the papers every day. Very stressful.'

'The thing is,' said Jon, we are all getting a bit fed up reading all the shit that is out there about this job. The bollocks that has been written. It's unbelievable.' We want to tell the real story, the actual story and what really happened, do you know what I mean?'

'Yeah,' I said. I was trying to keep the tone casual, but my heart was racing, nerves jangling. 'I know what you mean, must be really annoying reading a load of shit every day about something you know the actual truth about.'

I seemed to have passed their first round of vetting.

There was one thing that they wanted to be crystal clear about at this point, though. They wanted to tell the real story and were not bothered about money. According to them, they had piles of letters and offers but it was me they trusted to make a truthful book and film. I did question their assurances in my mind, but I parked the thought for now. Given the massive restrictions from the Proceeds of Crime Act, their apparent lack of materialism was music to my ears, for the time being anyway.

I reciprocated by outlining some of the offers and options. When it comes to telly, we could do a scripted or a non-scripted piece of work. Non-scripted was dodgy, though. I was imagining terrible scenarios where I accidently get them in further trouble by interviews incriminating them and me being in possession of those rushes with a legal obligation to hand them over to the police.

'I reckon it needs to be a drama not a doc,' I said. 'A doc would be too risky, I don't want to get anyone in any *more* trouble.'

Thank God they agreed. Jon suggested Ray Winstone as being perfect to play Danny Jones: 'Same age, from the same neighbourhood and he would get him just right.'

What channel though? We talked about Netflix and Amazon, the huge but relatively new entrants to the market who, now, everyone wants to both make things for and watch.

'Thing is,' I said, 'the ITV heartland audience for a drama could be 6 to 8 million people. Not many people have actually got Netflix. It's still mostly great marketing. I reckon we should do it for BBC1 or ITV. At 9pm and pull in close to 10 million viewers.'

They seemed to get it. There was a really positive vibe when we said our goodbyes afterwards. It hadn't felt as cloak and dagger as I'd expected, and while they were cautious and had been burned before, they were communicative, reasonable and pleasant. It wasn't the first or the last preconception I was going to see turned on its head during our strange encounters.

I had got everything I wanted from the meeting and, late into the night, I headed home light-headed and very excited to describe it all to my intrigued wife Emma. She started to keep a detailed journal of my recollections.

GETTING ACQUAINTED

The next day sobriety settled on me in more ways than one.

Were they playing me?

When feedback from Danny and Terry arrived via Jon after the meeting, it settled my shredded nerves slightly. I had passed my first big test. They were positive and felt it all to be moving forwards in the right direction.

Doubt had started to creep in that they might try to sell their story to the highest bidder, happy to spin any wild yarn to get hard cash. They were robbers after all!

They had given me some big ideas, though. I knew this story was dynamite, but I hadn't been thinking on the same scale as them. They wanted a Hollywood movie, a Netflix series. The way they were talking, it would be a challenge to satisfy them.

I started asking around to see if anyone would be interested in joining forces. After a few disappointing knockbacks, hope arrived when the Head of Drama, Myar Craig-Brown, at the production company Wall to Wall, mentioned the megastar drama writer Jeff Pope to me. However, he was top of every head of drama's wish list for factual drama and she indicated that we were unlikely to get him.

As luck would have it, though, I knew him. Jeff and

I were connected via his great friend and my former colleague, supporter, mentor and good mate on *The South Bank Show*, Daniel Wiles. Since those increasingly distant days, Jeff Pope had gone stratospheric.

In 2012, *The Guardian* published their top 100 media power list and a new entrant joined the list at number 91 – Jeff Pope. Aged 50 at the time, Jeff had recently finished executive producing ITV's most acclaimed drama of the previous year, *Appropriate Adult* (starring Dominic West as Fred West), which swept the boards at awards time. This chilling story of Fred and Rosemary West deeply affected me when I watched it. His later drama of that year, *Mrs Biggs*, which he executive produced and wrote, debuted on ITV with over 4 million viewers.

His previous work included working as executive producer on the 2006 ITV drama about the Moors Murders, *See No Evil*, and, in 2010 on Channel 4's acclaimed Mo Mowlam docudrama, *Mo*. Early 2017 saw the transmission of the smash hit *The Moorside* with the brilliant Sheridan Smith for BBC One, with Jeff again working as executive producer.

In 2013 Jeff hit another level co-writing the screenplay of the movie *Philomena* with Steve Coogan. It earned them an Oscar nomination. The former writing partner to the late, great Caroline Aherne, the favourite writer of Sheridan Smith, Jeff is allegedly looking at how to bring the life of Jimmy Savile to life in a TV drama.

Jeff Pope is quite simply the top of the tree when it comes to factual drama. His gift for investigating, writing and producing the most engrossing and engaging stories means that he always entices the best actors to work with him, too. I couldn't think of anyone more qualified to write this Hatton Garden drama. The prospect of writing to Jeff and seeing what he thought of working together on the idea was so exciting that I cut the meeting with Myar short and rushed out to email him.

Several of my colleagues assured me that asking Jeff to write my Hatton Garden heist drama for me was a great idea, but warned me that he took six weeks to get back to people. It was hard not to smirk when he replied to my exploratory email within 24 hours.

Hi Jonathan

Good to hear from you. I am definitely interested in meeting. Have been working myself on this story so maybe there's a way to join forces.

*Let me know when is good. I can do end of this
week/most of next.*

*Best
Jeff*

We called a meeting.

I knew before the meeting that Jeff Pope and his trusted producer Terry Winsor were the way to go, but the meeting itself still left me buzzing.

We agreed to meet where he works (and I used to work) at the London Television Centre on the South Bank. There I met a distinguished-looking grey-haired fellow of about 60, Terry Winsor. Terry is Jeff's drama producer. We talked for about 15 minutes and waited for Jeff, who appeared with an assistant. A lift whisked us all up to the 14th floor where we gulped coffee and brainstormed. Jeff Pope's tall good-looking son George, who works for Jeff, was there too.

Jeff lasered straight in on the importance of the timeline. *What happened minute by minute? Whose job was it?*

Jeff had devoured and processed what was already out there, the good, the bad and the utterly absurd, including the in-depth piece that *Vanity Fair* had published about the robbery, primarily from the police perspective. He also scoured the books that had been rushed out about the story, as well as press cuttings and police transcripts in the public domain.

He and Terry had quizzed the police, the solicitors, the vault owners, the neighbours and jewellers who work cheek by jowl. Where I knew things first-hand that he didn't, I filled in the blanks.

His timeline was impressive but still full of holes. He hadn't had any access to the guys themselves. They wouldn't talk to anyone. They had ignored every letter any film company and production company had written.

This is where I came in. Despite knowing so much, like the pro he is, Jeff was tormented by what he didn't know. So they sent me off with a stack of tricky questions to put to the gang, and we needed honest answers.

It was time to sort another meeting in our Enfield pub.

This time they seemed more money-motivated. Whatever conversations had taken place with the Hatton Garden gang after our first meeting, now cash was driving them.

The only real money I had in the bank at this stage was Jeff Pope. I laid out who he was and what a big splash he could make at ITV with the idea. Val knocked back a drink and started showing me shots of Danny on her phone. I was getting little stories out of her now, piecing together what kind of a man the charismatic Danny Jones really was.

We left on good terms but even so it was no surprise when a text landed from Jon.

'Spoken to Danny and Terry. They want promises. And definites. They are prepared to work with you but you need to tell us exactly what they will get and what it will be. Plus they weren't impressed with ITV. They want Netflix or Amazon. They wouldn't mind a feature film but they need convincing that ITV is big enough.'

Back at ITV, it was time for a second meeting with Jeff, Terry and George. We went to the restaurant Canteen under the Royal Festival Hall and against its noisy, clattering background, fairly unafraid of being overheard, we talked it all through. Jeff was gently teaching me what was to be a very important lesson on my journey about not taking anything at face value, especially from an extraordinarily cunning band of thieves. I couldn't assume that everything I was getting from the gang was true.

The ultimate result of this was me going back to Jon

and Val and laying it on the line. An ITV drama with Britain's greatest factual drama writer was the best option but we should do a book too. A feature film could follow the success of the drama and book, and, yes, that could involve megabucks.

Val was pleased, impressed even. I was keeping her on side. Sufficiently intrigued, or maybe just with dollar signs flashing in his pupils, Jon assured me that he would speak to Danny and Terry and they would agree with the book collaboration and, unsurprisingly, the shot at a future mammoth movie deal.

More than ever at this second meeting, it was coming home to me that this was Danny Jones' story. Sure, it was his common-law wife giving me the inside track, but that wasn't the whole story. The famous Brian Reader was hardly getting a look-in in their version of events, and as we all knew, Basil was a ghost, having disappeared into thin air.

Danny was at the epicentre not just of the heist itself but of all the planning and the aftermath too. I had to wring out everything he knew.

This story turned from news headline to legend in less than a year. But it was Jeff who encouraged me to use my head and think about who was actually behind this myth-making. For every factual correction, there was another story that didn't hold water.

Danny had bought the critical second pump – the tool that enabled them to push over the metal cabinet containing the safe deposit boxes after they'd drilled through the vault wall – in Val's name. He had signed it 'V Jones'. The police and the press thought he had been pretending to be Vinnie Jones, and the *Vanity Fair* article has followed this line. However Danny hates Vinnie Jones and all wannabe hardmen fakes, and the V stands for his beloved Val not the ex-footballer and fake gangster Vinnie. That quality of insight was what I was after.

But the Belmarsh Danny Jones wasn't coming to me so easily. When Jon did go back to Danny and Terry, they weren't sure. Sticking to their guns on wanting Netflix, they didn't seem to grasp the scale of the ITV, book deal and movie proposal.

While I was working out my next move on this messy chessboard, it was time for me and Jeff to broker a deal. I updated Jeff, and reminded myself I was the only person with an inside track to the robbers in Belmarsh and to Val and Jon. I had to keep the faith.

GETTING ACQUAINTED

And it worked, as I met Jon and Val regularly over the coming months before our meetings eventually tailed off.

To win over Jon, Danny and Terry all over again, I needed to know what made them tick. It was time to dive into the murky depths of where the whole heist began and establish what happened from the key figures in the story themselves...

CHAPTER THREE

NUTS AND BOLTS

'It's the biggest robbery in the fucking world.'
(Terry Perkins)

How was such a brazen plan concocted in the first place and what does it feel like during the planning? How exactly did the gang all meet? Whose job was it? Who first came up with the idea to get into this vault? Which one of them brought the team together, and which one of them was mates with the elusive and highly skilled Basil? These were some of the very first questions that I wanted answered. I'd get what I was looking for during the course of over a dozen meetings with Jon and Val, two other close gang associates, and senior figures from the police.

Danny Jones says that the original plan was to get in straight away and to clear the place out. Everyone would be a pair of hands. Then they would go and lie low somewhere. Possibly Southend.

Terry, a diabetic, had conscientiously brought along three days' supply of insulin, which, given how long the job ended up taking, turned out to be a near-fatal oversight. The plan was rigorous, detailed and professional; each man had a clear and distinctive role to play. The core gang members carefully constructed a tiny circle of trust, or at least they tried to.

So who were these gang members? It's worth reviewing the rogues' gallery before we delve further into the nitty gritty.

INDEX OF GANG MEMBERS

Danny Jones
Age at time of robbery: 58
Connection to the other gang members: old friend of Terry Perkins
Known criminal past: imprisoned for five years

in 1982 at Snaresbrook Crown Court after stealing £92,000 worth of items from Ratner's jewellery. Other suspended sentences for activity dating back four decades including robbery, burglary and handling stolen goods.

Physical appearance: fit, healthy, stocky build. Cropped white hair, strong jaw, remarkably unlined face, perhaps down to his teetotal lifestyle.

Key character traits: persistent, shrewd, keenly aware of the value of everything, loyal to his friend Terry and his family.

Quirks and distinguishing features: a showman with a strong sense of mischief.

Terry Perkins

Age at time of robbery: 67 (celebrated his birthday during the heist)

Connection to the other gang members: friends with Danny for decades and his virtual neighbour, living a mile or so away in north London. Danny lives in a lovely house situated along a row of flashy homes in the Enfield area. Terry's nearby street is more modest, comprising Victorian cottages and 1930s semis.

Known criminal past: 22-year prison sentence for stealing nearly £6m in cash during the armed robbery of the Security Express vaults in 1983. This raid also happened to take place over an Easter weekend. After a decade, he broke out, only to be caught again in 2012. He had been recently released before the Hatton Garden heist and was looking for one more job.

Physical appearance: cropped grey hair, set, thin lips, watchful blue eyes, drinker's roseate complexion.

Key character traits: hugely loyal to his old friend Danny. Likes clarity and having things explained properly to him. It's family first for Terry, who attends his granddaughter's ballet recitals and is largely motivated by helping his family financially somehow.

Quirks and distinguishing features: high level of self-awareness, which he often contrasts with the slowness or delusion of other gang members.

Brian Reader

Age at time of robbery: 76

Connection to the other gang members: long-term associate of Terry Perkins and the man who brought Basil onto the job.

Known criminal past: 1983 conviction for the Brink's-Mat gold bullion armed robbery at a Heathrow Airport warehouse. Imprisoned for eight years for conspiracy to handle stolen goods and assisting in disposing of the gold bullion after the multi-million raid. He received an extra year of jail time for a further conviction of dishonestly handling £66,000 in cash.

Physical appearance: short white hair, full lips, still tough-looking though also increasingly physically frail.

Key character traits: the Guv'nor, a natural leader with a commanding presence and a decisive attitude. Thorough and methodical to the point of obsession.

Quirks and distinguishing features: sometimes written off by other gang members due to walking off the job. Despite his illnesses and personal troubles, there was plenty of bite and menace left in Brian when he felt that he needed to bring it. His whole life, he has never been one to easily relinquish control, but he is also the ultimate pragmatist.

John 'Kenny' Collins

Age at time of robbery: 75

Connection to the other gang members: the first of the Hatton Garden gang that Danny called. Brought in as the lookout and getaway driver.

Known criminal past: served an 18-month sentence in 1975 for handling stolen goods (31 dresses and two skirts). Also a failed attempt to defraud a Post Office in 1978. Some low-value burglaries including breaking into a shoe shop, much to Danny's amusement.

Physical appearance: thick-set, sandy grey hair, thin-lipped, vacant expression. Ruddy and liver-spotted facial complexion.

Key character traits: not very bright. As Danny puts it, 'he is full of gangster-isms, isn't he, Kenny.' Prone to laziness, creating many funny moments during the police surveillance when his unwillingness to even walk his dog became a running joke.

Quirks and distinguishing features: tendency to fall asleep at critical moments. Slow on the uptake and finds it difficult to keep up with other crime members when plans are formed.

'Basil'

Age at time of robbery: late 40s / early 50s

Connection to the other gang members: Brian Reader brought him onto the job.

Known criminal past: unknown

Physical appearance: ginger hair, or possibly a ginger wig.

Key character traits: the 'alarm man' and much more. Detailed technical knowledge.

Quirks and distinguishing features: everyone laughs

when we discuss Basil and clearly know a lot more than they are letting on.

Carl Wood

Age at time of robbery: 58

Connection to the other gang members: Carl had been friends with Danny for over 30 years after meeting in a pub and sharing an enthusiasm for fitness. He was also in dire financial straits, leaving him very vulnerable to persuasion.

Known criminal past: none. Carl was subsisting on bits of decorating and DIY work where he could get it. Danny said of his desperate plight, 'fucking going to work for 20, 30 a day. Broke his finger the other day. Fell down a ladder.'

Physical appearance: balding with brown hair, wears glasses. In the words of *GQ* writer Stuart McGurk he 'looked like a particularly mendacious traffic warden.'

Key character traits: tough, with a ferocity born of desperation.

Quirks and distinguishing features: Carl had suffered from the chronic pain and discomfort of bouts of Crohn's disease since his mid-20s. This had granted him a fortnightly disability allowance of £320 but he was still £22,000 in debt, and married with two children.

Hugh Doyle

Age at time of robbery: 48

Connection to the other gang members: Terry, Danny and Carl knew Hugh from down the pub. They had been drinking buddies for years and his rather anonymous Enfield premises struck them as a natural meeting and hiding place. They used his plumbing business, Associated Response, as their rendezvous point. They stored much of the less valuable gold and gems in his yard for several weeks after the robbery.

Known criminal past: none

Physical appearance: wiry, fit and healthy.

Key character traits: polite and a gentleman throughout, and a showman in court.

Quirks and distinguishing features: he wore a T-shirt with the logo of his plumbing business on it throughout his trial as a rather misguided attempt at 'free advertising'. Obviously operating on the principle that no publicity was bad publicity.

William 'Billy the Fish' Lincoln

Age at time of robbery: 60

Connection to the other gang members: Jon Harbinson's uncle. Brian Reader claimed never to have met him before and he was unknown to Danny and Terry.

Known criminal past: small-time villain usually in a supporting role to bigger hitters.

Physical appearance: grey-haired, paunchy, heavily lined face.

Key character traits: always tries to be helpful.

Quirks and distinguishing features: like Kenny, physically in poor condition and tires easily. Gained his nickname from his friends at Porchester Baths, where he liked to sell fish he had brought from Billingsgate Market.

Jon Harbinson
Age at time of robbery: 42

Connection to the other gang members: Billy Lincoln's nephew. He was a taxi driver, which is why the gang considered him potentially of use.

Known criminal past: none, and was ultimately cleared of involvement in the Hatton Garden robbery.

Physical appearance: slim build, pale skin, receding dark cropped hair.

Key character traits: a very unlikely criminal and, after being cleared, found it difficult to cope with the stress and anxiety induced by his involvement in the case.

Quirks and distinguishing features: told the jury at the trial 'it's a bit of a pattern for me. I fall out with people.' He had been estranged from his uncle for 20 years before they reconciled.

Pooling their knowledge and tribal loyalties, the raid took over two years of meticulous planning. Although it didn't suit Danny and Terry to acknowledge it later, Brian's expertise had certainly fed into every stage of the planning. What had not been planned effectively was the very thorny and incriminating question of where the loot would be stored afterwards.

Danny doesn't trust people easily, to put it mildly. He is fiercely protective of his family and his privacy. Terry is the same. A doting father and grandfather, Terry cherishes his daughter Terri. Terry was vigilant from the very beginning of the plan about allowing her to get too close. In the planning stage, Terry made it very clear that he didn't want her to burdened by association with the loot or with Brian Reader.

As early as August 2012, almost three years before the robbery, Danny Jones was searching the internet for drills. By May 2014, a year before the robbery, Danny's googling had focused in on the drill that they used the first night, the Hilti DD 350 drill. By January Danny was having regular planning meetings with Terry and Kenny at The Castle pub in Islington.

NUTS AND BOLTS

It was that same month that Lionel Wiffen, a jeweller who worked in 88–90 Hatton Garden, started to have the funny feeling that he was being watched. Instinctively vigilant, Lionel and some of the other Hatton Garden jewellers had noticed some vehicles making repeat appearances in the street, with occupants who appeared to be casing the joint. Certainly Terry's blue Citroën Saxo, later to play a headline role in the police surveillance, was right in the vicinity of Hatton Garden on 13 February 2015, not long after one of his regular meets with Danny at The Castle pub.

As I said at the start of this story, Danny is more important in this planning than anyone has indicated before.

Danny and Terry go back 20 years, to when they first met in prison in Blandtyre House. Blandtyre House is a category C/D resettlement prison housed in a converted stately home near Goudhurst in Kent. It was taken over by the Prison Commission in 1954. Originally founded to imprison young offenders, it later became a resettlement prison for long-term prisoners. So, Danny and Terry came together in prison and have been proper friends ever since. What Danny and Terry actually wanted out of the Hatton Garden robbery was relatively modest.

Transcripts from the undercover surveillance operation reveal that Danny was involved just because he wanted 'enough money to pay the bills next week'.

Ever the family man, Terry had them in mind with his share: 'What I wanted out of this was to…' Terry started.

Danny, as he so often does, finished Terry's sentence off for him. '…give your kids a house each.'

'Yeah, which is out the window now,' said Terry ruefully.

'Yeah,' Danny agreed regretfully.

'And I would like to get another flat out in Portugal,' Terry continued. 'To rent out for the business thing.'

'Good money it would make, Tel,' Danny agreed. Danny is never one to miss a business opportunity either.

'Mate, yeah in the season you get a monkey a week for it,' Terry exclaimed enthusiastically. 'Well the season is three months, you make… you wouldn't make any money to live on but you'd make say five or six grand a year, it pays all your exes and all your holiday and all that.'

'Yes,' agreed Danny.

Terry continued, 'And for the future you ain't never going to make money in property in Portugal for about ten to 15 years. So I'll never see the profit.'

'No,' said Danny. 'So that would solve your problem.'

There is something rather poignant about this exchange. It certainly doesn't sound like two greedy criminal masterminds gloating to each other, but two tired old men worrying about life's minutiae and how to bankroll them. It recalled to me the words of Martin Amis from his aptly titled novel *Money*: 'Money doesn't mind if we say it's evil, it goes from strength to strength. It's a fiction, an addiction, and a tacit conspiracy.'

From childhood onwards, Danny was a guy who always wanted more. As a boy Danny Jones stole some copper and managed to sell it on. He realised at that point that he could make money from stealing and he was hooked. He began to take it seriously, like a profession, a vocation, his calling. He has never looked back, and consequently, has never done an honest day's work in his life.

A major part of the reason this book came about initially is that Danny wanted his story to be told. The more I was told about Danny, the more his exploits and personality gripped and captivated me. I asked Val and Jon to pitch an idea to Danny that we would, following this book, look into writing a 'young

Danny'series of adventures about how he had got into the unusual and remarkable life he had led in the first place. Val and Jon agreed it was a brilliant idea. They would put it to Danny. I would turn Danny into a literary hero, a modern-day Robin Hood, although perhaps without the 'giving to the poor' bit. I received a message back via Val that Danny wanted Terry to be involved in any enterprise like this. Out of loyalty to Terry, Danny didn't want a series of adventure books. He wanted to do a book about him and Terry.

Val met Danny through her brothers when she was 16 years old. She grew up in Edmonton, north London and Danny was her brothers' mate. Val and Danny have two children together, one grown up and one teenager.

Val has described Danny as an incredibly controlled guy. She says that he hates to drink and doesn't touch drugs, because he always wants to be in control. His favourite beverage is tea with honey in it.

Naturally gregarious and curious about his fellow men, he always has time for people – the elderly ladies near where they live love him and he always stops to talk to them when he is going on one of his long runs.

Danny is obsessed with exercise and physical

strength, which came in very handy indeed during the breaching of the security vault. Danny and Val have had many a good laugh over the extremely unflattering mugshot of Danny, which always appears in any press article about him.

Val has shown me quite a few pictures of Danny in which, to be fair, he is a very handsome and stylish-looking guy. He loves adopting different personas and guises... Jon gave some examples where Danny pretended to be ex-SAS and another time when he played the part of a Russian oligarch at an ultra-upmarket watch convention.

Danny sometimes tries on different personae during run-ins with the law, too. He described an extraordinary situation when he was pulled over without a licence... except maybe a poetic one.

"I ain't got no licence, have I" My name was on the insurance but they didn't know that. "What's your name, what's your name, the copper kept asking me." I said, "Mind your own fucking business; I want to talk to your partner, not you. He's more professional." The copper started laughing. He spotted the army rucksack I run with in the back of the car and he went to me, "What you got that big bag for?" I told him, "I'm in the Army. I help teach squaddies how to survive in

hostile territory. I said I'm flying out actually today."
He went, "Fucking put it there mate and fuck off. Get
your mate to pick the car up, alright?" I said "Cheers"
and scarpered.'

Danny also takes a certain pleasure in his canny
ability to hide loot.

He bragged to Terry about one ingenious place he
had come up with: the light fittings in his house. 'Good
hiding place, Tel!,' Danny remarked.

'Yeah,' Terry returned, admiringly.

'Fucking yeah,' Danny grinned.

'If you're putting your gear there, don't tell me,'
Terry said.

Danny needed Terry to have his back, though. Just
like always. 'I've got to tell you in case anything goes
wrong, fucking hell! If anything happens to me, it goes
to Val.'

Danny was as keen to make provision for his beloved
Val's uncertain future as he was to keep her well away
from his criminal activity and gains.

As always, Terry knew the wisdom of not knowing
too much.

Terry and Brian have worked on some of the biggest
robberies in British criminal history. Brian helped

to launder the gold bullion from the £26 million Brink's-Mat job in November 1983 for which he was imprisoned for nine years for conspiracy to handle stolen goods and dishonestly handling cash; Terry was involved in the £6 million Security Express robbery in April of the same year and was caught and convicted two years later for 22 years. The other gang members pay due deference to these two, with Danny Jones especially aware of their history – perhaps even slightly hero-worshipping them. But Danny is a serious career criminal himself, committing armed robberies on his own. Carl is a hard man, used for his brawn and brains, and was brought onto the job by Danny. Carl's history shows that he'd be the one to deal with anyone who got in their way during the break-in. And he was paid a wage not a split of the take. Maybe Danny bunged him some cash after the robbery to buy his silence, though.

Brian Reader's rap sheet was characterised by his past criminal association with the notorious Kenny Noye. Brian had gangland connections in a way that Terry, and certainly Danny and Kenny, largely didn't. In Kenny Noye's garden in January 1985, police surveillance officer John Fordham was murdered. He was stabbed multiple times in both the back and chest. Brian Reader was also charged, although in the end both men were acquitted on the grounds of self-defence. Kenny Noye is currently in prison for a 1996 road rage murder on a slip road of the M25, when he stabbed 21-year-old electrician Stephen Cameron to death in front of his girlfriend. Kenny Noye had mounted a bid in early 2017 to be moved to an open prison.

It didn't take me long to pick up on a distinct rivalry between Brian Reader and Terry. The rivalry between these two men is central to the story and an integral part of why the plan unravelled. They share a love/hate relationship, with Terry resenting Brian's high-handed manner and assumption that he is the top dog, having carried out similar high-profile robberies in the past. Some were successful and others not. This rivalry is at the heart of the ITV drama and provides the spine of the story.

In Danny's view there was a rivalry between him and Brian too. Furthermore, Danny had detected the rivalry and peculiar relationship that existed between Brian and Terry.

As Danny commented to Terry about Brian, 'Everything he says, he ain't as fast as you. So every time he just shuts up. If he comes back and he gets a point from you, he goes "yes, yes" in celebration.'

'Yeah,' Terry concurred.

Danny explained that he didn't enjoy those situations, saying, 'I get more pleasure laying there with my fucking old dog', although in fairness to Brian, there are few things that give Danny more pleasure that spending time with his beloved dog.

'It's true innit, it's fucking true,' agreed Terry, aware of Danny's adoration for his pet.

Danny sighed wearily. 'He wears me out Tel. No need for him to wear me out no more though. We have done all the dog's work, ain't we?'

Terry folded his arms. 'He ain't never going to work again, and please God, we ain't either! Just sit back and that's it.'

Danny leaned towards Terry confidingly. 'He is jealous as fuck of me, Tel, did you know that?'

'He is, yeah,' Terry concurred vehemently.

Danny carried on. 'He is jealous of the youth, the age, the jobs you can go on.'

Terry raised his own jostling for position with Brian. 'Yeah and he knows my history, I've been on better bits of work than he'll ever fucking do.'

Even so, Brian and Terry, both lonely in their own ways, did spend time together. Brian's wife Lynne had died six years before the robbery, in January 2009, aged only 65. This had left him bereft, a bit lost and purposeless. Maybe her death had fired his sense that he still had it in him to do one more big job, which would give him a welcome distraction from bereavement and boredom.

Brian had become even more curmudgeonly, as Danny said, 'He's got a bad fucking problem. I bet he's one cunt to live with.'

'Oh dear,' was Terry's response, sympathising with Brian to some extent.

The Castle pub in Islington was their favoured place to hang out, along with their adored Italian haunt in Clerkenwell, Scotti's Snack Bar. The Castle pub is rather evocatively situated at 54 Pentonville Road, and a little part of Brian and Terry enjoyed the irony of meeting in such close proximity to one of Britain's most famous prisons.

The Castle has a lovely roof terrace with panoramic views of the Angel district of Islington, but Brian and Terry generally preferred to cloister themselves inside. With real ales and a traditional layout complete with bar stools and small tables, The Castle is a bit of a haven as an authentic boozer in one of London's most changeable and try-hard-trendy areas.

Scotti's Snack Bar in Clerkenwell is perfectly suited to these two old criminals and it became their regular

Friday thing. Like them, it is part of a vanishing breed and a waning British institution – the humble caff. A cosy little white property with a blue awning, it is nestled unassumingly in a part of Clerkenwell that whilst expensive and chic today, was gritty, industrial and urban when the men were young. With seating and décor that has barely altered since the 1950s, it is the perfect place for a real cup of tea, a crispy bacon and egg fry-up, and a quiet chat reliving their old criminal heydays, bragging about who they've met, the characters they've worked with and, of course, the jobs they've pulled off.

That's not to say that Terry always enjoys Brian's company, though. As Danny remarked to Terry during one of their post-heist chats: 'He's really getting on my nerves now, Brian. Fucking wearing me down.'

'It's repetition of the same old shit,' agreed Terry.

'Argumentative that old cunt,' grizzled Danny.

'Yeah,' Terry concurred.

'He knows he ain't getting a dollar.' Danny was standing firm on this point.

Terry shrugged. 'He knows it now, if he don't he is a cunt. He's still hanging on though, ain't he?'

'Yeah, he ain't got nothing else,' explained Danny.

Terry knew that whatever their differences, Brian

leaned heavily on him for human company. 'If I ain't there Friday, where's he going to go, he's going to go home, ain't he?'

'He ain't got no friends no more,' Danny exclaimed, feeling a sudden rush of pity for the old villain.

Unlike Brian and Terry, Danny isn't so keen on self-indulgent reminiscing. He's a man of two modes: relaxation or action. He prefers to be at home drinking tea with lemon, taking the dog out or running.

Terry and Brian live alone, several gang sources have confirmed. Terry was closest to his daughter Terri, who was also involved in the robbery, having laundered some of the loot. They don't know much about his other kids except that they really don't think that Terry is particularly close to them. However, one thing Val said at our very first meeting was that it was always very separate – they would never all go for drinks or for a meal for instance with other gang members. She just knows them as people Danny works with.

Danny and Val are extremely discreet about their views on the personalities of the accomplices, but Danny's taped conversations with Terry are considerably more frank, revealing a high degree of scepticism about the mental faculties and street smarts of both Billy and Kenny.

One key point that came out from all my conversations was that Basil was involved in the job from the outset. He was not just the outsider brought in for the alarm as the police originally appeared to indicate. The gang admitted to me that he was a main player and as such was due an equal share of the loot.

Certainly Brian knew about the Hatton Garden vault and the 1975 robbery where armed raiders had gained access via the lift. But it was Basil who had the keys and knew about the alarm.

The next gang member, Kenny Collins, was primarily brought in as the look-out and driver. Kenny and Brian had contacts in the jewellery trade. Kenny has convictions for fencing stolen property. He is the common contact between the Danny and Terry camp and Brian later in my story.

Kenny was to become a key player in the storing of the loot too, and Terry and Danny had him earmarked for this role from very early on. However, Kenny failing to make adequate arrangements was a common conversational theme amongst the gang.

As Terry said, 'What ain't going to happen is everything being sorted at once. It ain't happening, it ain't fucking happening. It'll end up being Tuesday, cos he ain't made arrangements. He ain't gonna bring it Monday, is he?'

Danny's typical response was to try to be practical. 'Tell him to come over Monday.'

'So are you going to phone him or me,' Terry sighed with exasperation. 'Bloody Kenny. Bloody logistics'.

'You phone him,' Danny mumbled.

'I'll tell him to what, pick you up?' Terry enquired gruffly.

'Yeah, tell him to pick me up, what time, Monday?' Danny ventured.

'It don't matter to me,' Terry snapped back.

'Ten o'clock?' Danny tried to calm Terry by sticking to the basics.

They sorted the rendezvous at Sterling Road. They could sort Kenny out then.

The police reckon if the heist was Danny's idea, he would use Brian and Terry because he knew he could trust them. They were old school and would No Comment if they were arrested. Or so Danny thought…

CHAPTER FOUR

AND SO IT BEGINS

'You gave up being a thief ten years ago, you cunt.'
(Terry Perkins)

Exactly how the heist started is as gripping as any part of this whole extraordinary saga. The way that the gang broke in and how Basil managed to avoid detection really captured the public's imagination. Even more so, everybody loves an underdog and it is impossible not to feel sympathy for Danny and Terry as they describe exactly how gutted they were when all their dreams seemed to lie in the dust when the pump broke at the end of the long first night.

The devil's in the detail, and some of the details I learned about the preparation for the job were truly surreal. Brian borrowed someone's Freedom Pass (a contactless Oyster card allowing people over 60 and the disabled free travel on public transport in London), which he registered under his long-term pseudonym, Mr T McCarthy, to get to the job. Danny wore his mate's son's red shoes for the job, much to his partner Val's shock and amusement. Dapper Danny borrowed a Montana '93 American football top from the gym just for good measure, too.

Val has talked to me a lot about Danny being very short-fused in the run-up to the job.

'He was bad tempered around the house. On edge. As you would be.'

Not that she knew why or what was going on, of course.

Gang associate 'Arthur' explained another important aspect of the planning to me. 'All of them were paranoid about phones. They knew that was an easy way to get caught later.' I agreed that it certainly was, and it had ended up forming part of the police investigation regardless.

Arthur went on that 'You have separate "burner" phones in the run-up to and immediately after a job, but you then go back to your usual phones.' He was convinced that this common criminal practice had been deployed by the gang.

Another gang associate told me that the original plan was to get in straight away on the first night and open as many boxes as they could in one hit. Then to go away for the weekend. Possibly to somewhere like Southend, and just lie low in a seaside boarding house with all the other bank holiday mini-break crowds. Hence Terry bringing three days of insulin with him. Everyone would be a pair of hands. But despite best-laid plans, things didn't quite work out this way.

They say that you can't teach an old dog new tricks. But Danny and Terry were to prove themselves more than capable, with the help of Brian and Basil, of updating their skillset from the good old early days of their criminal past.

Back then, as Terry said, 'Going back 30-odd fucking years we had an open back truck cos it was the right fucking thing to do. And we done jobs on a Saturday morning at fucking 10 o'clock!'

Danny tried to butt in with 'under everyone's…'

Terry was on a roll, though. 'We pulled up like fucking builders and slung the rubbish in.'

Now, though, they needed to be squarely in the modern age.

D-Day. Thursday 2 April 2015

Brian Reader left his Dartford home at 5.15pm and caught the 96 bus from West Hill School to Dartford Station. Then, at 5.48pm, Brian caught the train from Dartford to Waterloo East, arriving just after 6.30pm.

At this point, I am told that Basil was already outside either number 88–90 watching, or at a lookout point opposite at number 25 Hatton Garden in a first-floor corner office. I've been told both things and I'm not sure which is true. However, having looked at both spots, either would have given him a good vantage point to see both the jewellery dealers with their wares and the activity of the security guards. Security Guard Kelvin Stockwell was preparing to secure the premises for the duration of the bank holiday weekend.

Meanwhile, Danny was driving the white van with Terry sitting beside him in the front passenger seat. They picked up Carl en route. The van contained a lot of important kit including high-visibility jackets, hard hats and overalls.

The last customers at the vault were gone by 6 pm, and that was the regular cue for Stockwell to lock up the vault. Carlos Cruse, the building co-ordinator, could see Stockwell and the other guards preparing to secure the premises on his CCTV.

Carlos also checked the basement and courtyard. The alarm was set, and Cruse closed and locked both doors of his office. After waiting for the security guards to leave the building, he activated the magnetic glass door in the foyer. At 6.05pm, Carlos left through the main wooden doors to 88–90, which locked automatically.

Nine minutes after his arrival at Waterloo East Station, Brian caught a bus to Holborn. At 7.02pm Brian arrived at Hatton Garden on the number 55 bus and strolled down towards the vaults. He wouldn't have aroused much suspicion; he was just another smart, older white-haired gent in that part of London.

At 7.30pm, Danny, Terry and Carl met Kenny Collins, who was driving the van. They had walkie-talkies at the ready. They loaded two wheelie bins into the back of the van.

As Jeff Pope and Terry noted, 'Significantly there is no street CCTV of Brian or Basil at this point.' One of the questions I had been mulling over for months and months, and batting back and forth with Jeff and Terry, was who brought Basil onto the job. Whose man was he? I badly needed a breakthrough on this mission-critical point. In late winter 2016 I got one. First came a clue from Val. She said to me, 'Danny and Terry had never even met him before.' Later I received confirmation from gang associate 'Arthur'.

'Brian Reader brought Basil onto the job, Jonathan. Basil was Brian's man'.

At 8.23pm, with Kenny driving, the white Transit van arrived and parked in Leather Lane. All the gang members except Kenny went to the van to dress in their high-visibility jackets and other gear. Kenny gave Danny a walkie-talkie and ear piece so Danny could communicate with him.

Unfortunately poor old Kenny couldn't get the hang of the walkie-talkie. They had completely forgotten to do a lesson or a test with the communications. Kenny was treating it like a phone, answering 'hello' when someone was trying to talk to him. The others began to get frustrated.

The gang have mentioned that adrenalin was running high at this point and they found it comforting to focus on mundane tasks like dressing and sorting the walkie-talkies.

At 8.28pm, Danny and Carl walked anti-clockwise round the block. Basil walked clockwise, with a black bag on his shoulder.

AND SO IT BEGINS

The three men then met up to sort some details on the corner of Hatton Garden and Greville Street, on the opposite side of the road to the metal fire exit door. Danny and Terry tested the walkie-talkies while Terry and Brian waited in the van. It was getting tense.

The day before had been cloudy and rather cold for early April, but 2 April had been warmer and drier all day. The sun had set at 7.30pm, and even with the lingering twilight and light pollution, the skies were dark as the remaining customers thinned out of Hatton Garden.

Hatton Garden jeweller Lionel Wiffen let his last customer in at about 8.30pm through the Greville Street metal fire exit door – the door that he habitually accesses his office from and opens for his customers when the main door to the building is locked. The only two holders of the keys to this Greville Street entrance are Lionel Wiffen and the staff of Hirschfelds, an antique jewellery shop that has been based in Hatton Garden since 1875. This door has two sliding bolt locks, one on the top and one on the bottom, which are secured from the inside, outside of opening hours. This outdoor fire exit key is the one key that Basil couldn't get hold of, so he would have to open the door from inside.

Meanwhile Danny and Carl were hovering by some phone booths with walkie-talkies and continuing to try and talk to the frustrated and flustered Kenny. The gang were starting to stress out about losing time.

At 8.45pm, Basil indicated that he should get a move on, grabbed a walkie-talkie and walked along Greville Street. In the first of many such cunning and shrewd moves, he used a black bin liner to hide his face from the on-street CCTV cameras. He was the only member of the gang to successfully conceal his face from the cameras for the entire job.

Basil opened the mortice night latch lock on the front entrance of 88–90. This was the door, which all building tenants would have a key to. In the foyer, Basil was faced by a glass door with a coded lock. Did he know the code or did he use Danny's electronic gadget to tell him the numbers? The police tell me that Danny owned such a device. However, it was also just about possible for Basil to bump the doors up and down until they separated.

Nothing makes Jon and Val close ranks faster than asking them detailed questions about Basil's methodology. Of course I wanted the answers, but I had to sail very close to the wind to get them.

When I asked Jon if Basil knew the code, he waggled

a finger at me in warning. Though his tone was slightly playful, there was steel right underneath it. 'Now you're getting very technical.'

Val had shifted uncomfortably in her seat. I didn't want to push it. Fortunately, other sources including the police surveillance were able to clear up many points without forcing Jon and Val to feel compromised.

In any case, they tell me that he entered the correct sequence of numbers.

At long last, at 9.21pm, and to everyone's relief, Lionel Wiffen locked up and left via the Greville Street metal fire door entrance. By force of habit, he was careful to make sure it was shut properly a minute later.

At 9.22pm the white Transit van turned into Greville Street, and Danny, Terry, Brian and Carl unloaded the equipment. Meanwhile, unwittingly put an hour behind schedule by Lionel Wiffen, Basil purposefully made his way to the Greville Street metal fire exit and let the others through from the inside. This provided us with our first tantalising glimpse of Basil on CCTV, and what a very odd glimpse it was. He was wearing a ginger wig, cap and face mask. When did he get changed into that get-up? Was he already inside or had he changed outside? Did he change at the look-out point at number 25? Either way, his street clothes were probably in the bin liner.

Brian was the first in. Characteristically Basil was very aware of the CCTV camera again, with his black bin liner at the ready as he headed back to the fire escape.

By contrast, the rest of the gang were oblivious to the cameras, at least it appears so from looking at the CCTV footage. Either they didn't know the cameras were there, or they didn't care. If it was the latter, as gang associate 'Arthur' has told me is likely, they simply reckoned that they could steal the hard drives away again later and destroy them.

Kenny drove the white van away and parked it roughly 200 yards away.

The rest of the team apart from Basil can be seen on CCTV carrying in equipment bags, tools and two wheelie bins, taking them all down the iron fire escape to the courtyard. This was the first of many onerous physical tasks for these ageing criminals. Maybe Basil was already on to his next task at this point.

In addition to his yellow hard hat and high-visibility jacket with 'GAS' on the back, Brian had brown shoes, stripy socks and a distinctive scarf that the police found at his home address during the arrests. Terry also sported a high-visibility waistcoat and hard hat, along with dark clothing and a white surgeon-style mask.

Just before 9.30pm, Danny hurried towards the van. He collected a green crate that he had forgotten and went back inside the Greville Street fire exit door, closing it behind him.

Danny and Carl carried the bulky wheelie bins down the iron stairs to the courtyard along with bags of tools and the acrow-prop, which would be used as a temporary support for the hydraulic ram and pump.

At 9.40pm Kenny appeared. He was wearing a green quilted jacket, a flat cap and was carrying a brown briefcase. He walked along the main Hatton Garden street. This could all be seen clearly on a shop's CCTV. He turned into the foyer of 25 Hatton Garden, but at first the key didn't work properly and he couldn't get in. After a bit of fumbling, the key worked successfully. Kenny let himself into a corner office on the first floor. Once in position on the first floor, he had a commanding view of both entrances: the main entrance of 88–90 and the Greville Street metal fire exit door. This was to be his look-out position.

The walkie-talkies worked fine outside but it is unlikely that they would have worked in the subterranean vault, buried under thick layers of industrial concrete. They were mainly used so that Carl could communicate with Kenny while he kept watch overlooking the courtyard, providing muscle if needed as well as an extra pair of eyes.

Basil had a key to open the door for the stairs leading down to the basement beside the lift. That way, he was able to open the basement fire doors in order to let everybody into the vault and to drag in the wheelie bins.

Over the months, one of the questions I was trying to find the answer to was who had the inside track on the vault. Who knew where the alarm was, where the locks and cameras were situated? After some polite fencing at our second meeting, I worked up the courage to ask Val directly. She genuinely didn't seem to know, answering, 'No clue,' and shaking her head apologetically.

Jon was watching me searchingly and also waved the question off with 'You're getting a bit technical now…' There was a warning tone to his voice. I had to back off.

Next, I tried 'Arthur', crouched in a corner of a deserted Enfield pub. I know him well enough to know he always sits in the same corner, but I doubt anyone else ever notices him as he carefully blends into the background. What would happen if any silly punter tried to take his regular seat is anyone's guess though. 'Arthur' was more forthcoming. He leaned in, as usual rather enjoying speculating about the extent of the endless ingenuity of some of his more creative criminal friends.

'Just say if one of them had arranged for a mate to be a prospective customer a few months before the robbery and open a box there. With regular visits that would give you plenty of insight, wouldn't it?'

Chief Detective Superintendent Tom Manson had already shared the police theory with me that Kenny Collins allegedly visited as a potential customer, and that this could also have been to put his prints at the scene for a reason. In the same conversation, Tom had made reference to reports of Terry Perkins, disguised in blue workman's overalls, casing the building prior to the burglary.

I leaned in a bit closer to 'Arthur'. 'Do you really think that might have been what they did?'

He shrugged. 'I would if it was me doing it'.

This was just a theory, sure, but it was a plausible and entertaining one. He carried on.

'Come on. Think about it. Maybe one of them might have known someone at the company that fitted the alarm? There are ways of getting to know somebody too, you don't need a mate on the inside every time. Pay someone off. None of the regular fuckers in these places get paid shit, do they? Doormen, security guards, alarm fitters. Nice little earner if you approach with caution.'

I pushed it further but he clammed up. That was as much as I was getting on that subject.

The basement fire door to the courtyard has two sliding bolt locks, one on the top and one on the bottom, secured from the inside. So, wheelie bins and equipment may have brought in at this stage and it may be that's what Basil went off to do as the rest of the gang brought the gear down the iron staircase to the courtyard. They'd re-lock the basement fire door to the courtyard after they'd brought all the gear inside.

At about 10.10pm, Basil and Terry went to the second floor. They called the lift. Terry pulled the door sensor off so that the door stayed open.

Then came a crucial moment. For the first time, Basil seemed to slip up. He and Terry can clearly be seen on CCTV standing by the lift, but the ever-vigilant and crafty Basil does not seem to be aware that he's been caught on camera.

The gang have told me that they didn't get the lift

ready in advance at the right floor. It was too risky. I asked the same question of one of my police sources for his views on whether they got the lift ready before the job – when Lionel Wiffen was there? He responded, 'No knowledge, but a risky plan if they thought someone was in the building that late; suggestion is Basil had the access.'

The gang tell me that Danny forced the lift doors open on the ground floor and dropped down the lift shaft all the way to the bottom – some 12 feet. Then they carefully shut the lift doors behind them again. I am desperate to know who wrote the note that they left on the lift saying 'out of order'. The gang are amused and I am told that it was Terry. This is something that the police don't know. In fact one source said he thought that 'it was never resolved; it may have been Lionel Wiffen when he returned to clean during the weekend.'

It is striking to me what an even division of labour there was between the men in many ways – pretty democratic despite their varied ages and abilities.

It was Kenny, who had gone with Danny to purchase the second drill in Kenny's white Mercedes, and this whole second phase saw him generally get in deeper with the job. Along with Terry's blue Citroën Saxo, Kenny's white Mercedes was to have star billing in the later police surveillance.

Because Basil had a key to open the door for the stairs leading down to the basement beside the lift, he was able to open the basement fire doors to bring in the gear. As 'Arthur' laughingly pointed out to me on this point, 'Otherwise his only option would have been the mad one of opening the lift doors and scrambling back down the lift shaft again. Impossible!'

Prosecutor Philip Evans QC aptly described the situation with the lift during the trial at Woolwich Crown Court. 'So there they are, inside Hatton Garden. The lift car had been moved to the second floor where it had been disabled: the door sensors had been left hanging off so that the doors would remain open. This opened a short drop down the shaft from the ground floor to the basement. At the bottom, the shutters were then pulled open from the inside. They were buckled. On the ground floor, a handwritten note had been stuck next to the lift, which had not been there before: it said, "Out of order".'

Basil took the cover off the electrical box underneath the security desk which powered the outer sliding iron gate and cut the wires. This cut the power to the gate and allowed it to be pulled open. The gate was magnetically locked and mechanically opened. It's a sliding iron gate, which is right in front of the inside of the main entrance wooden door to the Hatton Garden vault. It's hard to imagine that Basil would have been capable of knowing all this without inside information and having worked there himself, a theme I will return to later.

But as DCI Tom Manson rightly pointed out to me, there are different degrees of insiders. It's hard to say how many different people would be privy this information, but it's probably more than you'd think. After all, think about all the people that go in and out of that place. All the contractors, customers and staff over the years. Hundreds of people.

Even with all this wizardry though, Basil didn't totally disable the alarm. At 12.18am, the alarm triggered a text message alert to the monitoring company, indicating that the outer iron gate had been opened. The gang did this so that Carl could nip out and use the walkie-talkie. Fortunately for the gang, this mistake did not bring the whole plan crashing down.

The owner of the vault's son, Alok Bavishi, received a call from the monitoring company almost immediately. He was told that the alarm was signalling and that the police were on scene. We know the latter part of the message was wrong: the police never came. Alok Bavishi rang Keefa Raymond Kamara ('Ronald'), but the trains had stopped running and he was without a car, so he could not attend. He then rang Kelvin Stockwell: the call initially went to voicemail but after a few minutes it connected: he spoke to Stockwell, who agreed to go to Hatton Garden to check the building.

Alok Bavishi himself was not originally intending to accompany him, but then decided he would as Stockwell was by himself and the police had been called, or at least he thought they had. Stockwell arrived at Hatton Garden at about 1.15am; he called Alok Bavishi, who was by then five minutes away, to say that the main door and the fire exit appeared secure. Stockwell informed Bavishi, wrongly, that it was a false alarm. Both men returned home, as the attempts to access the vault, unbeknownst to them, continued inside.

Philip Evans, prosecuting at the trial, gave a succinct account of what happened next: 'Uninterrupted thereafter, the men spent the night cutting through the second sliding iron gate and then drilling three adjoining and circular holes in the thick wall of the main vault with the Hilti DD350 drill they had brought with them and left behind. Their efforts left a 25 x 45cm breach in the wall. They would, at this point, have encountered the back of the heavy metal cabinet housing the safe deposit boxes which was fixed both to the floor and ceiling. It appears that they had with them that first night a Clarke pump and hose, which included a 10-ton hydraulic ram.'

Down at the bottom of the lift shaft, Basil was holding a torch so the other gang members could see their way. Camera footage of the shaft shows they also had some fluorescent lights to help them see, but as they tell me, 'It was an insurance policy.'

It wasn't easy to get through four inches of a bolted metal shutter, but the air jack they shoved into the gap, plus some exhausting pumping on the handle, got them in with a loud crack. 'Once the shutter was separated from the bolts it could be slid up easily.'

At about 10.30pm that night Danny got out again through the Greville Street metal fire escape door and emerged onto Greville Street. He walked towards 25 Hatton Garden, keeping in touch with the gang inside on his walkie-talkie.

'Alright. No alarms going off outside here.'

Inside, the men were in the 'airlock' between two metal security gates.

Terrifyingly, Basil had just one minute to disable the alarms, which were tucked away in a cupboard under the stairs. In that 60 seconds he managed to do some very clever stuff. He cut the grey telephone line cable coming out of the alarm box, broke off the GPS aerial and deliberately damaged the keyboard.

Kenny might have described Basil 'baffling him with bullshit' about the alarm, but beyond a bit of showmanship, Basil undoubtedly knew his stuff and came into his own, and all the other men respected him for it.

I asked one of my most high-ranking police sources, Tom Manson, about this crucial 60 seconds. He told me that Basil seemed to know a lot of detail about the security inside the vault, such as the knowledge that they had only 60 seconds to disable the alarm and that it was located in the cupboard under the stairs. 'How do you think he knew some of this fine detail?' Tom remarked.

Tom told me it, 'could have been he was a customer or had details from another customer. Although there was no evidence of an insider from the owners at the time, I'm not sure how far back the team went on previous owners or people who had access to the building. Also not every owner of every box came forward and many could have used false names…Basil appears to have the missing link…'

Even so, much later when the trial was underway at Woolwich Crown Court, a security guard was willing to testify under oath that, in his view, this had to be an inside job. Kelvin Stockwell, having worked in the building for more than 20 years, agreed with defence lawyer Nick Corsellis' suggestion that the burglars must have had 'inside information'. Kelvin confirmed that he was notified about alarms going off very early in the morning on 3 April, but found everything in order when he visited the site to check.

Nick Corsellis asked Kelvin, 'But it is plain to you, is it not, having worked there for as many years as you have, appreciating the complexities of the security system, where things are located, how things were bypassed, what area of the vault was drilled into, that the people who were involved in this crime must have had detailed inside information to commit this crime.'

The next obstacle was a large wooden door secured with a mortice deadlock. Danny made pretty short work of the lock and broke it open. That allowed them to start to bring their wheelie bins and tools down into the vault. Basil opened caretaker Carlos Cruse's office. There was an inner office door that was padlocked. It was down to Basil to break it open.

Maybe at this point Carl was able to keep an eye

on the whole area through the CCTV cameras in the caretaker's office. Now and then he would go out to the courtyard to call Kenny on the walkie-talkie. Kenny was finally getting the hang of it.

Danny started cutting through the sliding metal gate with an angle grinder, trying to get into the vault itself.

It was the opening of this door that triggered the automatic text message to the monitoring company, the Southern Monitoring Alarm Company, despite Basil deactivating the alarm. So at 12.18am, a computer screen at a security centre in central London registered an alarm being triggered at 88–90 Hatton Garden.

Two minutes later the Southern Monitoring Alarm Company contacted the Metropolitan Police's Central Communications Command. Alok Bavishi received a call from the monitoring company and he was told that the alarm was signalling and that the police were on the scene. Something we know did not happen.

Understandably, for public relations purposes, Scotland Yard were compelled to release a statement addressing the confusion over the police response. They laid out the facts in a brief statement.

'At this stage we have established that on Friday, 3 April at 00.21 hrs a call was received at the MPS Central Communications Command (MetCC) from Southern

Monitoring Alarm Company. The call stated that a confirmed intruder alarm had been activated at the Hatton Garden Safe Deposit Ltd. The call was recorded and transferred to the police's CAD (computer-aided despatch) system.'

Now came the embarrassing, and baffling, part of the statement: 'A grade was applied to the call that meant that no police response was deemed to be required. We are now investigating why this grade was applied to the call. This investigation is being carried out locally. It is too early to say if the handling of the call would have had an impact on the outcome of the incident.'

Bavishi rang Kelvin Stockwell but, unsurprisingly given the hour, the call went to voicemail at first. A tense few minutes later, he got hold of Stockwell and told him to get down to Hatton Garden. Thinking on his feet, Bavishi decided to go with Stockwell, and of course both of them were wrongly expecting to find the police on the scene too.

At 12.50am, poor Kenny, stuffed full of fish and chips and very tired and stressed by everything, fell asleep at his look-out post with his walkie-talkie sitting on his ample tummy.

In Danny's words, 'Funny fucker is Kenny.'

Terry couldn't agree more. 'Kenny is! One hundred per cent funny fucker!'

Val says one of the things Danny talks about when looking back on the robbery is how unintentionally funny the whole thing was, particularly the famous moment when Kenny was meant to be look-out and went across the road, got fish and chips, ate it and fell asleep. They kept radioing him and he wouldn't answer. Eventually he answered as if the walkie-talkie was a telephone again with a 'Hello, who is it.' In Danny's memorable and genius, if rather ungenerous, manner of speaking, 'Kenny is a wombat-thick old cunt.'

Meanwhile Carl can be seen in view of the CCTV camera by the top of the basement stairs next to Greville Street fire exit. He waited for a moment and then went back down to the basement, listening out for alarms going off.

He called Kenny on the walkie-talkie and in no uncertain terms woke him up. 'Sorted Kenny? Everything OK?'

The CCTV camera in the fire exit passage was owned by Berganza Jewellers. It was movement-activated and didn't record every journey past it. It only really seemed to activate if someone was hanging around directly outside the door. In other words, it might not have picked up on plenty of gang activity even as they were hovering about near it.

According to the insight of one person very close to the gang, they all thought that they had disabled that Berganza CCTV camera already, but they continued to turn their heads away from it out of instinct.

Ridiculously, for our elderly gang, the adrenalin of this critical point in the heist wasn't enough to stop Kenny from falling asleep again. And as he slumbered, oblivious, Kelvin Stockwell rocked up at 12.15am.

Stockwell went and inspected the main Hatton Garden entrance. He tried the doors and of course found them all still locked.

Kenny woke up and saw Stockwell prying about. 'SHIT.' Kenny jumped up and frantically contacted Carl, who was wandering about the courtyard, on his walkie-talkie. Stockwell was getting warmer now, approaching the Greville Street metal fire escape door. Shit!

Carl hadn't been selected for his pretty face. He had a violent reputation and despite his painful Crohn's disease, he was very much the muscle in this scenario. Carl could be aggressive and unpredictable, with a short fuse fuelled by his physical suffering.

But what no one wanted, least of all Danny, was for

Carl to have to use this muscle in anything other than the hypothetical.

On this basis, they made the difficult decision to get out. They could see the security guard was about to come into the building, with the police no doubt not far behind him. They abandoned the vault. They abandoned their tools and they headed as stealthily as they possibly could to their only possible escape route, the iron staircase leading up to the roof.

But providence intervened. Just as he was about to unlock the main doors, Stockwell got a call from Bavishi. 'I'm five minutes away. Don't go in there on your own, Kelvin, wait for me and the police to back you up.'

In any case, Kelvin was thinking it was a false alarm. An hour had gone by since the text message alert had come in. There was no sign of the police about so maybe they had already been and gone, having found nothing of interest.

Stockwell rang Bavishi back. He said that the main door and the fire exit looked secure and there weren't any alarms going off in the street. 'False alarm,' he said. On the basis of this misinformation, both men went off home again.

This series of errors could not possibly have been anticipated by the gang but what a gift they were. It took a while for the gang to believe their luck though. The coast was clear? Carl wasn't going to have to rough anybody up? He was very relieved.

At 1.30am, 'jittery and fucking knackered' the gang went back to work inside the vault. 'Let's get this fucking thing done.'

Danny continued cutting through the second sliding iron gate with an angle grinder, and bent up the bars to gain access to the operating mechanism at the base of the gate – another act that suggested they had inside information. Eternally 'switched on', Basil sat at the security guard's desk by the vault entrance. Watching, watching, always watching. His laser focus was on the control panel for the CCTV system which covered the airlock and the vault itself.

At just after 2am, they were drilling three adjoining and circular holes in the thick wall of the main vault with a Hilti DD350 drill. The gang tell me that the drill had to be bolted to the wall. Danny and Terry prepared the water supply, used to cool the drill, in a bucket. Apparently if you are an expert you could drill through the wall in 45 minutes BUT the drill has to be bolted to the wall in three separate positions. Danny had studied the manual and it said: 'The drive unit must always be mounted on the drill stand when in use and the drill stand secured adequately by means of an anchor, vacuum base plate or quick-release brace.' The gang tell me there was dust everywhere and it was dirty and stressful. They were getting splitting headaches from it all. Basil was quiet, silently and forensically playing his part, displaying little interest in anything directly outside his 'official remit'. Funny bloke, the gang tell me. For all his good work he seems to have got Danny and Terry's backs up a bit though. Maybe this was because he was slagging them off, taking the piss out of the diamond wheezers and playing the big man about his status as alarm man and hacker extraordinaire. Perhaps that's why Danny and Terry were pretty critical about him messing up the alarm.

After three hours of back-breaking and incredibly frustrating work and, an almighty mess of rubble and dust around them, came a moment of ecstatic relief. The third hole was finished. The bloody thing was 10 inches high, 18 inches wide and 20 inches deep. A huge hole to dig, but not a huge hole to crawl through.

Terry paused to give himself the insulin injection he needed for his diabetes. Danny glanced at him, concerned but glad he seemed to be keeping on top of things.

AND SO IT BEGINS

The incidents with the late closure of the premises and Stockwell snooping about had thrown the gang's best laid plans and tight schedule out. It was 4.30am, they were knackered, and the dust was stuck in the back of their throats.

How was everybody feeling at this point, was the question I wanted put to Danny and Terry. The answer that came back was pretty simple.

'Fucked off. Tired. And we hadn't even started to put together the air ram yet, the part where the pump was going to push the cabinets away from the wall. Or we hoped it would. We just kept pumping.'

'Why aren't the fucking cabinets moving?' they asked each other hoarsely. Fuck!

They kept pumping. And pumping. After about an hour and a quarter of this nightmarish activity, true disaster struck. With a loud bang, the pump, slipped, then gave way completely and shattered irreparably into pieces.

No pump = no vault access = no loot.

They needed a bigger, more powerful pump to apply pressure, and what they had, abruptly and crushingly, was no pump at all. They were screwed.

Danny and Terry played this black moment over endlessly afterwards. They were feeling their age, the back-breaking labour, the ungodly hour on a bank holiday weekend.

They turned on Brian. Why the fuck hadn't he thought that the cabinets might be bolted to the floor? He was meant to know about this place. He had co-ordinated the job. He was meant to be the fucking Guv'nor!

This played straight into one of Terry and Danny's key anxieties about Brian, based on bitter past experience – his basic competence.

Recollecting a previous occasion, Terry said, 'He carried one thing in there, he diddley'd and doddley'd about and then it was all in. He's not a thief!'

Danny agreed wholeheartedly. 'Yeah, he's a liability, he never carried one thing out, did he, Tel?'

'No, not one thing, he carried fuck all.' Terry nodded.

Danny knew the crime landscape they faced today was a very different one to the one in which a young Brian Reader had managed to gain such a formidable reputation. 'He was a thief forty years ago, they never took no chances, had it all their own way. Like all them thieves then. All that fucking business, all his partners, and all that, they weren't worth a wank. He's done nothing, the cunt, you would think he would shut up, Tel.'

AND SO IT BEGINS

'You would think he would be shut up with shame but he's not ashamed of nothing,' shrugged Terry.

Looking back on it later, nobody could really say whether the intention was for Brian to crawl through the hole if they had managed to get in that first night. After all, the Guv'nor was the one that seemed to really know how to open the boxes quickly, but he would quite possibly have been too big to fit through. This was something that could only have been answered if Brian had been there to attempt the hole himself, or if someone with a virtually identical physical frame to him had given it a go.

In reality they couldn't get in and they hadn't expect to hit as much metal in front of them. So they needed a bigger, more powerful pump to apply pressure.

'It's because you didn't align the pump properly and broke the base,' Brian spat back. Brian doesn't take any shit despite his age. Carl was seething menacingly. This wasn't how it was meant to happen. Carl was still angry at the near miss with Stockwell which hadn't been meant to happen either. This wasn't good.

Terry called Brian out, told him he didn't bone up on it all the way like he should have done. He told him he was useless and missed obvious massive problems despite being a self-styled master criminal. There were so many simmering tensions between the gang members bubbling up now. Most of all Danny and Terry's feelings about Brian.

As Danny said of the situation shortly afterwards, 'I really want to have a go at him but I've got to stop myself. Really want to hit him and say toughen up, you old prick, you fucking prick, that's what you are. You lost all the fucking work, you bottle out at the last minute.'

Terry agreed with Danny, based on bitter experience of what Brian was, or perhaps better to say wasn't, capable of. 'I'm going to tell him about his three bits of work for this job, I fucking gotta tell him, I can't help it. I am going to say you fucked every one of them up, Brian, and the last one you walked away from.'

'Every one,' agreed Danny contemptuously. 'You're supposed to be a full-on thief!'

'You gave up being a thief ten years ago, you cunt,' Terry snorted of Brian.

'More,' said Danny, as always egging Terry on.

And it worked, because Terry was boiling over: 'You didn't even look at the front door, you didn't take the right drill in and this one you fucking walked away from. If we had took any notice of you we would have walked away from it as well… we would have walked away, we had no other bit of work, and in three months' time you would have got £400,000 for your house. That's how much you were fucking worried about it. And that is the fucking truth, the basis of the matter.'

Back in the vault, the gang was imploding at the speed of sound. They stood in the hellish environment they had created, squabbling. There was no organised plan anymore, nothing planned for this totally unexpected contingency. They hadn't thought to bring another pump. Major mistakes had been made and there was no obvious way forward. Basil didn't have any ready answers for once, either. The unit was in total disarray, freefall.

Seasoned and aged Brian Reader's gut instinct kicked in. Suddenly everything seemed crystal clear to the old rogue. Walk away. Don't get caught. There will always be another opportunity, and if there isn't then at least you're not lurking about waiting to get caught for this botched job.

Terry and Danny stared at Brian in amazement at this revelation. 'What?!'

Terry shook his head. 'Mate, we've been planning this together for years.'

Brian held their gaze. 'Yes but we had a plan. It's gone wrong. Walk away.'

'We can cut our way,' said Terry. He suggested that they use an acetylene torch.

Brian shook his head, exasperated and furious. He raised his voice: 'This is how you get caught. You're panicking.'

Danny wasn't standing for any of this. He wanted to carry on. They were in too deep and had come too far to give up. There had to be a way. Basil, as always, was listening carefully but saying nothing.

Whatever the plan would be for the rest of the weekend, it was time for them to make themselves scarce. The sun would rise on this Good Friday at 6.32am. They prepared to take some stuff out but left the wheelie bins behind. The gang tell me that they sprayed all around with a special substance to get rid of DNA traces and soaked the tools they didn't take with them in bleach. It was also at this point that Basil very cleverly took out all of the computer hard drives containing the CCTV footage from both the vault and Carlos Cruse's office.

Between 7.51 and 8.06am Danny can be seen on CCTV footage toiling up and down the stairs with two holdalls. Terry, Brian and Carl pitched in hauling the equipment up the steps and leaving it all ready to be picked up by the fire escape. To say no one was in the mood for all this was an understatement. It's a type of work they all hate even when they've got loot in hand, let alone without it. But, with bitter irony, they never let go of their instinct not to get caught.

Danny and Terry stopped Basil from shutting up the Greville Street fire exit. Just in case. They were talking furiously between themselves. There had to be a way through this. Had to be. They couldn't come this far and give up. They weren't quitters. This was meant to be the big one. The final one. The job to end all jobs. Fuck. They had to do something to pull it back.

This nugget from Danny and Terry gives rise to the intriguing question of where Basil's loyalties lay at this point. The police transcripts seem to show that Basil was closest to Danny amongst the gang members. It seems clear that Basil had a lot of time for Brian too. The elder statesman, the legend. He had 20 years of experience on Basil and presumably several more high-profile robberies too. And I am told very reliably by the gang that Basil was originally Brian's man. It was Brian who brought Basil onto the job.

But when push came to shove, whose side was Basil on? Did he want to carry on like Danny and Terry or walk with Brian? As it turned out, he was up for trying again.

If Basil had the key to the door to the stairs that run from the basement to the ground floor foyer, then he used the stairs at this point. If not, he must have had to climb up the lift shaft. Either way, he left through the front entrance somehow. We don't know how because he dodged all the CCTV footage. Did he know how to avoid all the cameras or was he so brilliantly disguised that even the obsessive police scrutiny of the CCTV footage can't reveal who he was? It seems unlikely at that hour of the morning, with not that many people about. Maybe he got changed at number 25. We just don't know.

What we do know from the surveillance is that at 8.20am, he took the van to Kenny's house in Bletsoe Walk where he got dropped off with Kenny and Brian. Billy the Fish was there, too. Meanwhile, Danny, Terry and Carl were talking in the van about whether they could carry on without Brian, and more importantly in their eyes, Basil. Danny was convinced he could get inside.

A couple of hours later, Danny drove the van, Carl sat alongside him, to Enfield where he dropped Terry back home and then Carl at his place in Cheshunt.

AND SO IT BEGINS

Danny was physically and mentally shattered at this point, but his mind was still whirring. He wasn't going to quit. No way. Not after all this. This job was the one. The big one. He was going to sort everything out for himself and Val and everyone he cared about. Got to get the job done somehow.

Billy gave Brian a ride back to London Bridge Station in his Audi, dropped him there at 11.18am and that was it. Stepping out of the car, Brian Reader was out of the Hatton Garden job. Good riddance thought the others. However, Brian was troubled. This could all still go very wrong if they tried to carry on without him... but they wouldn't dare, would they?

CHAPTER FIVE

PROBLEMS

'I am 67. Fucking 20 pills a day... yeah, if I don't take insulin for three days you'd have to carry me out in a fucking wheelie bin...' (Terry)

As I learned in new detail from the gang themselves, the big conflict at the heart of the robbery was Brian Reader walking off the job. On the first night they tried to get the loot and it failed. Brian said, 'Forget it, it's over. We are gunna get caught. It's done.' This created all the subsequent rows and tensions during the job, and it is what was behind the majority of the bickering after the job was done. Ultimately it was the carelessness and chatter because of how angry they were with Brian that led to them being caught. Although, of course, the sophistication of the police surveillance also came into play.

When Brian Reader gave up, the gang was livid. Danny and Terry, if they had ever been that impressed by Brian's Guv'nor routine, were heartily sick of his shtick now. They were left unsure as to whether he had ever fully planned to go through with the scheme, at least in the terms on which they had planned it.

'He had a back-up,' said Danny.

Terry was riled. 'A back-up, I can't get over him, the cunt, he's done me out of fucking money.'

Danny sneered, 'Everything he has done and he's the "master criminal".' Danny disparagingly accompanied the last two words with the 'scaremarks sign' from his index fingers. 'Everything he has done has fucked up,' Danny sniffed dismissively with a wave of his hand.

It was Terry, though, despite having sometimes vouched for Brian in the past, who was the first one to consider cutting him out of the deal. In the end Terry and Danny insisted on cutting him out. And there was no way were they giving up on the job.

'Fuck him,' Terry said. Then the most significant three words in this whole job: 'We're going back.'

PROBLEMS

On the afternoon of Friday, 3 April, Danny was keeping a close eye on the news. Had they been discovered yet?

There is then a gap in activity that no one seems to be willing to explain to me. Was Brian crying into a pint somewhere, thinking about what a failure it had all been? Also, we don't know what Basil's feelings were at this point, although we can have a pretty bloody good guess. Obsessively cautious, surely Basil would also have agreed that this was the moment to throw in the towel.

What we do know is that Danny and Terry were plotting their next move, and plotting it fast. The two of them met over at Danny's house. Naturally, they talked about what kit they needed and what the plan of action was. Danny rang Carl to talk through the plan with him and to see if he had any fresh ideas.

A definite part of Danny and Terry's new play was that Basil was not going to be allowed to fade into the shadows that easily. Brian 'could fuck off'. However, they needed Basil not just to get into the building, but to get through the hole. Terry could try to sweet-talk him back in while they were out buying the pump.

It was Kenny who rang Machine Mart on Saturday 4 April to ask about a Clarke pump and hose. This was not a result of Danny and Terry scheming and colluding to give Kenny a potentially very compromising job. They just felt they could trust him with it, and that it was a good idea for him to have something to occupy his mind. Everyone was massively stressed. A simple job for Kenny seemed like a good thing. That's not to say Danny and Terry were beyond having a chuckle about poor chubby Kenny, half-deaf and struggling through everything. The police transcripts show them talking about Kenny getting on in years and forgetting stuff, except when he really needs to remember, of course.

In all the access I have had over the last year or so, nobody has ever criticised Kenny directly to me. They are very loyal in that sense. They are not happy that their intensely private banter about other gang members has been put out there in the public domain, just like you and I would be unhappy if every chat we had about our friends or colleagues behind their back was recorded and leaked.

Kenny collected Danny and drove him to Twicken-ham to buy the second hydraulic pump in his white Mercedes. When it came to entering the shop, though, only Danny went in. There's CCTV footage in D&M tools at 4.30pm. The Mercedes can be seen parked outside. Danny didn't buy anything.

PROBLEMS

Danny then went next door to Machine Mart and bought the Clarke pump in Val's name. There is an invoice for a Clarke pump made out to V. Jones, Park Avenue, Enfield, Middlesex – he left out the number but that was his real home address. Val knows exactly how important this was and talks about it to me obsessively. The police, of course, later traced this pump purchase. They managed to connect Kenny and the Mercedes and also then used it to identify Danny.

Back in the Mercedes, Danny used Kenny's phone to speak to Terry for a while. Danny also then gave Carl a ring to tell him that it was game on all over again, and to sort out collecting him for round two at the vault later that evening.

Then there is a bit of a mystery. Kenny's Mercedes journeyed first to Islington and then to Enfield. Given Danny's silence to me on what was going on at this point, I suspect the trip to Islington was to pay Basil a visit. Danny would surely have gone in person to get Basil back on board at this critical point, to get him on-side again. The only other possibility is that they were trialling the new pump they had bought, but I don't know why Danny would be shady about that. Anyone with a brain in their head would want to make sure the pump was effective this time way before they were taking the huge risk of heading back in the vault with it.

What's more likely is that they tried out the new pump in Enfield afterwards, where Kenny also picked everybody up and took them back to his house at Bletsoe Walk.

At 8pm, Lionel Wiffen and his wife Helen arrived at 88–90 Hatton Garden to clean their workshop together. Lionel is in his seventies, but still slim and tidy with a phenomenal work ethic even after 30 years in his Hatton Garden business.

Lionel noticed immediately that the Greville Street metal fire exit door was not only unlocked but ajar. Understandably unsettled by this, and wondering if there had been a break-in, he checked the fire exit basement door only to find it bolted from the inside and showing no signs of anybody having forced their way in. Satisfied that there had not been any intruders on this basis, Lionel and Helen double-checked that the Greville Street metal fire exit door was locked and headed off.

There is an intriguing little puzzle around the gang's timings at this point. They didn't rendezvous at the same time as Thursday night, this time heading back to Hatton Garden considerably later. Did they know Lionel and Helen were going to be there later that night, and if so, how? Whenever the gang goes silent on me my thoughts and instincts turn, rightly or wrongly, to Basil. Was Basil watching again? Was Basil enough of an inside man to have a sense of Lionel's timetable?

In truth, they do tell me that they were shitting themselves: they had got lucky the first night with the alarm, but that was a very close call. They have really emphasised to me how tired they were, and very jittery with everything that was going on, on top of sleep deprivation. They were feeling their age.

Also, Brian had scarpered, the rest of them were tired and they hadn't planned the next stage properly. At this point they were running on energy and determination rather than focus. As far as they knew, the police might have discovered the mess from the first night and they could be walking into a trap. They waited for ages outside before going in, watching and waiting. Seeing if anything was amiss.

I wanted a second opinion from Tom Manson, with his decades of experience, to put his head into the minds of the villains and tell me what he thought was going through their brains in the immediate lead-up to the second attempt to get into the vault. Tom thought and then summarised it in four distinct points: 'Prior arrangements, getting everyone in place, situation around the venue, bottle'.

What he was referring to was logistics. Sorting the new pump. Getting vehicles to get back to Hatton Garden. Making sure everyone travelled undetected and that each man knew exactly where they needed to go and what role they had on the job. A thorough recce and a search on arrival to check the Old Bill weren't lying in wait in parked cars, blacked-out vans, or by high windows with vantage points. And finally, summoning up the courage and sheer balls to go through with it all over again.

Certainly some kind of signal went out to the gang, as they waited tensely at Bletsoe Walk, because they drove to Hatton Garden pretty much the moment that Lionel Wiffen vacated his premises. What doesn't add up is that they had Basil, or someone, carrying out proper live surveillance on Greville Street at this point, so it would come as no surprise to the gang that Lionel had locked the gate. However, the fact that he locked the gate seems to have taken the gang aback a bit.

Regardless, Kenny's Mercedes was prowling out of Islington just after 9.15pm. Twenty minutes later a CCTV camera captured him parking in Leather Lane.

PROBLEMS

Kenny waited on the corner of Leather Lane and Greville Street and went straight back into his look-out routine, in which he had displayed such variable competence the first time around.

Danny and Carl walked past the Greville Street fire escape door and headed to the main entrance of 88–90. Alert to the slightest noise or warning signal, they were assessing the situation, and casing the joint, as effectively as they could. Having done so, they went back to the Mercedes. Once again, the CCTV footage that would prove so invaluable in building the case against them caught the Mercedes making its way back out of Hatton Garden.

Everyone's nerves were jangling, Danny and Carl most of all. Having to return to the scene of the crime was far from optimal, and Brian Reader had provided a bit of grizzled eminence and an extra pair of eyes whether they cared to admit that to themselves or not. Going back to the vault wasn't a given for these men. It was taking a huge risk. Brian might have actually been the one to walk away, but God knows it had crossed everybody's minds. Lionel and Helen's little visit had freaked them out even more, and left them wondering whether the Greville Street fire exit was secured or not.

The vehicles tell an interesting story here. An automatic plate number recognition camera on Clerkenwell Road clocked the Mercedes. Then just after 10pm a camera on Cropley Street near Bletsoe Walk recorded the Mercedes returning towards Islington. The automatic plate number recognition on Clerkenwell Road also recorded the white Transit van, driven by Kenny, arriving and parking on Leather Lane just like it had the previous Thursday night.

Danny, Terry and Carl exited the van and hung around in Greville Street opposite the metal fire escape door. Lo and behold, it was at this moment that Basil reappeared, with a bin bag slung over his shoulder, like the clichéd picture of a robber lugging a bag of swag.

Basil expertly opened the main wooden doors to 88–90 again and disappeared inside to deal with the glass foyer doors just as he had done before. Once again, Basil had somehow evaded any of the CCTV cameras in Hatton Garden until the moment of the break-in itself. Was this guy a magician?

I did find out from a gang associate that Basil had a mobile phone with him during the robbery. They couldn't say what kind. This associate reiterated the important point though, that most of the surveillance recordings were done by probes in the cars and the Castle pub, and that none of the gang members talked much on their phones.

The enigmatic and disturbingly skilled Basil really came into his own on this return visit. Basil had the front door key and he knew where every alarm, camera and motion sensor was. They told me at one point that when they were in the vault, Danny noticed a laser on his chest and thought it was a camera. Basil reassured him that it was a motion sensor. How did Basil know? Was he a Hatton Garden insider? A former policeman?

Meanwhile, Carl, who was much less calm and furtive than Basil, had been pacing the road to the Greville Street metal fire escape door and rattling at it a couple of times. The fact that it was locked really shook him up, so it seems like Carl at least was not privy to the information about Lionel Wiffen's visit to the building and subsequent locking of the side door. Without this critical piece of information to moderately calm his nerves, Carl's imagination was running wild. Were the police waiting inside, primed to pounce on the hapless group of old lags?

Carl had had enough. 'Let's sack this off. It's too fucking risky. Let's go home,' he said.

Danny did his best to steady him. 'Basil will be here

any minute. He just needs to come to the side gate and let us in.'

The minutes ticked by, the wait for Basil crackling with tension. Carl was jumping at every noise, especially the distant sirens and alarms that go unnoticed as London background noise by law-abiding citizens immersed in their own business. No sign of Basil. Carl was at the end of his tether.

'Fuck this. I'm heading off. They've probably already got Basil. I'm not waiting about for the Old Bill to pick up the rest of us. How the fuck do we get into the vault anyway? Brian fucked the planning. He got it wrong.'

Terry wasn't above begging him at this point. They were already one man down. 'We need you Carl, at least give it a go – if we don't get in, we don't get in. But at least we would have gone down trying.'

Carl, only on wages rather than a share of the spoils, was having none of it and walked off with a final 'Fuck this.'

Now they were two men down. First Brian. Now Carl.

The residual anger felt by Danny and Terry at Carl walking off the job would bubble over in a savage discussion between Danny and Terry reminiscing about this point in the heist.

PROBLEMS

'When you think about it we must have been crackers, we got to be stone crackers,' Terry opened up to Danny.

Danny concurred wryly, 'Well Brian must have thought so and Carl; they went, didn't they? I thought you saucy cunt. When we talk about Carl we say "you cunt".'

Terry took Danny very literally and replied, 'You cunt.'

He went on: 'I thought you fucking yellow cunt. He would have been better off coming and sitting down and apologising and saying–'

Danny butted in, speaking in an imitation of Carl's voice, 'I don't deserve nothing.'

Terry mimicked Carl equally mercilessly: 'I've fucked my whole life up then, I just don't know what to say to you.'

'Can't believe what you've done, you've fucked yourself up, you've fucked us up.' Danny had a half smile now. 'If I was him I would take up drinking.'

Terry happily played along. 'And I'd get out of my nut every night.'

Danny had the final words on the matter for now. 'You can try five million times to make it right, but you can't.'

Back outside the Greville Street side door, just as Carl disappeared, Basil materialised out of thin air and let Danny and Terry in. Thank God. The hold-up was down to the very necessary task of checking out the building. Down to three men (Kenny would continue to act as lookout), they hauled their kit back down to the courtyard, and closed and locked the Greville Street metal gate behind them.

It was getting late. The men had never been so tired and strung out. At about 11pm Kenny let himself back into the vantage point in the first-floor corner office again at 25 Hatton Garden. They got the walkie-talkies fired up again, using them to maintain contact with Basil.

It was Danny and Terry who were determined to see the job through.

If Brian and Carl had lost their bottle, there were also some serious issues with Kenny.

Unbelievably, given the circumstances, poor Kenny fell asleep at his look-out post again and faced the humiliation of being discovered and awakened by hyper-competent and vigilant master thief Basil. Not his finest hour.

Kenny had got himself some fish and chips before he had fallen asleep again. They kept radioing him and he wouldn't answer. Eventually Basil went over to see what had happened and found him asleep and woke him up. Then Kenny didn't understand his walkie-talkie again and said, 'Hello who is it, can I help you?' when the rest of the gang tried to talk to him. It was like *Dad's Army*.

That said, Kenny's evolving role in the second night is interesting, and too easily glossed over and diminished by some of the other gang members, who would rather treat him as the new boy, the Ronnie Wood of the Rolling Stones.

If Kenny Collins was Brian Reader's man, then why didn't he pull out, too? Why did he go back? A gang member has pointed out that Kenny was only on lookout – both the first and second nights – so his risk was much lower than the others, with a greater reward if it came off, as he was entitled to an equal share. The same source also said that when Reader walked off the job, Kenny stepped up a little. Almost as if he was imagining himself stepping into Brian Reader's big boots. Sadly, he does appear to have been a very dim version of Brian.

Even though Kenny was in many ways Brian's man, one of my senior police sources reminded me of an important point when I was quizzing him about

Kenny: he may have been Brian's man, but Kenny did introduce Billy, and Brian was not happy about that.

Danny and Terry did what they do best at this point. They kept the faith and got themselves immersed in the job at hand to close out external anxieties. Picking up where they left off, they started the tense and painstaking set-up of the new hydraulic pump, securing it onto the wall directly opposite the hole. They were pumping the lever. By now, as their weary eyes on the clock confirmed, it was about 1am on Sunday morning.

Danny was encouraging Terry: 'Come on Terry, steady, steady' when he was handling the prop.

'It's heavy as fuck,' Terry was groaning, the process debilitating him.

The second pump was attached, and therefore came into direct contact with the cabinet, whereas previously it was against the wall. As the pump started to push into the back of the cabinet housing the safe deposit boxes, there was plenty of disconcertingly noisy creaking and cracking.

In one of the covert police recordings, Danny and Terry recollected these difficult moments.

Terry had clear recall of the pump moving backwards, which made him tumble backwards, so they put something down to stop the pump pinging back. After that, 'It stayed put and I thought, it can only go forward now, can't it?'

For an agonising few seconds, it looked like the new pump was going to break, too. But then, with a last crack and an almighty crash, the cabinet came away from the wall and revealed the Holy Grail. A clear route through to the vault. Through this nightmare phase, it was Danny and Terry who were determined to see the job through. Danny has talked about the terrible headaches they were getting when they were down there in the lift shaft drilling on that second night.

Only Basil and Danny were slim enough to fit through the insanely cramped hole. What we do know from police sources is that it was always the plan for Basil to accompany Danny into the vault rather than just being the alarm man.

There was only one posture that could be adopted crawling through the hole into the vault – Superman-style. Danny slid his arm into the hole and then wiggled his torso through. Basil and Terry supported his legs and he made a final thrust to pull himself clear. Super-fit and highly disciplined, Danny was up to the job. Basil was right behind him, squeezing through the minute and claustrophobic opening.

I asked about the hole and Brian Reader and whether he was meant to go in. The gang said he was far too fat. But then they made the point that before they had made the hole they didn't know exactly who could go through. Because of the nature of the drill, you have to start again to make the second and third hole; it's not like breaking down a door then everyone is able to go in. So the plan was to make a hole big enough to gain entry, then whoever could get through would get through. And that, when it came to it, was Danny and Basil, with considerable discomfort.

This was nothing though, compared to what was going on with Terry.

Danny says that there were several moments over the weekend when he really thought Terry was going to die.

In the worst of them, Terry with his dodgy heart, keeled over just outside the vault, as he was passing some loot through the hole. Despite his insulin injections, he was beginning to enter a diabetic coma. It was genuinely touch and go. Danny and Basil had to stop what they were doing, which was incredibly physically arduous and taxing in its own right, and help Terry out. At one point Danny had to help him out by injecting him.

Only able to smile about it down the track, Danny was laughing to Val about what he would have done if Terry had died on the job. Leave him in there and carry on is what Danny wanted to do, but Val was horrified. 'You can't do that Danny!'

He couldn't resist inserting a bit of dark comedy into the proceedings. 'It's my birthday today!'

Danny and Terry had some choice words for Brian and Carl at this point.

Danny snorted contemptuously of Brian, "The biggest robbery in the fucking world and if you listen to the MASTER... you walk away.' What a loss for Brian, they were thinking. We've got in and he's walked away.

There was little chance of tubby, diabetic Terry going through the hole.

Danny exclaimed back through the hole to Terry, 'We would have been here for hours, Tel, if you had got in that hole – you'd have cut yourself to ribbons!'

Terry agreed. He couldn't stop looking at the tiny aperture that Danny and Basil had somehow squeezed through to get into the vault. 'Fucking would have and I'll tell you something, the only way in there is the way you went in.'

They shared a rare laugh at the thought of Terry snapping selfies with Danny and Basil in the vault in the background and sending them off to Brian. Terry was still extremely frail after his dangerous blackout, though, and fear for Terry's life was part of what informed Danny and Basil's decision to walk away with so few boxes as a proportion of the whole.

On 3 January 2017, Jeff Pope got in touch with me, copying in Terry Winsor, to share the question that he couldn't stop obsessing over. It was the same one I had been grappling with myself. When or indeed whether, Danny and Terry told Basil that Brian was going to be a no-show for night two at Hatton Garden?

There seemed to be several different possible angles on this. Danny and Terry might have carefully failed to disclose the issue with Brian and simply informed him as a fait accompli when they were all back together again for the second night. Handling it that way would make Basil leaving the job pretty unlikely since they would have got him to the right place at the right time; this would have allowed him to tell Brian Reader later that he was unaware of his absence until he was already back on the job.

Alternatively, they might have gone to see Basil some time before Saturday night, to tell him that Brain was no longer on the job. Or they could have gone to see Basil during that time period but not told him the truth of the situation and just allowed him to think that Brian would be there.

Of course, there was also the possibility that none of these scenarios was accurate. It could have been that the conversation about Brian walking off happened in front of everyone on night one down in the lift shaft.

Reviewing the robbery a month after it had happened, Danny and Terry couldn't believe some of what they went through on that second attempt.

Terry was, with some justification, proud of his fortitude in the face of his disability, compared to the fitter and younger Carl who had deserted them: 'Carl, I looked at him and thought I'm fucking different.'

Danny had Terry's back. 'You know you are, don't you?'

Terry wanted to outline the reality of his diabetes. 'Think of it, three days, three injections. I had it all with me, my injections.'

Danny replied with affected disbelief 'You never?'

Terry nodded. 'Course I had to take them in there for three days.'

'What were they, in your pocket?' Danny enquired, seeing that his friend needed to talk this out.

Terry let Danny know he was right. 'Oh yeah I had them in a proper pack in me bag, yeah.'

Danny's resentment towards Carl's abrupt departure bubbled up to the surface. 'And you've got Carl, who's been on massive bits of work, screaming like a fucking pig.'

Terry was still on his diabetes theme: 'Yeah, if I don't take the insulin for three days, I could… you would have had to carry me out in a wheelie bin.'

'Fucking hell,' marvelled Danny. As much as anything else, there was precious little space in the wheelie bins as it was without a hefty corpse to factor in.

Much as Terry had got stuck on his diabetes, Danny was like a dog with a bone about Carl. 'He sees Brian walking away…' Carl seeming to take his orders from Brian even after he'd left the heist was one of things that had riled Danny and Terry.

As Terry then said of Carl's attitude to Brian, 'That's it and he thinks he's [Brian's] the Guv.'

Danny grimaced sarcastically, 'He's the Guv, he knows.'

PROBLEMS

Later on I would learn from the gang that Carl likes a spliff and a drink of an evening. He says it calms down his Crohn's disease.

The rest of the gang, being drug-free, weren't averse to teasing Carl about his proclivity for weed.

Mimicking Carl's voice, Terry would say, 'Oh, can I have a bit of money for some shopping?'

Danny instantly cottoned on, and joined in the fun, also mimicking poor Carl. 'Oh I need a bit of money for a bit of puff... fuck off.'

Kenny wanted to join in the merriment of the conversation but was slow on the uptake as ever 'What, for smoke?'

Danny chimed in impatiently, 'I said to him stay there, if we get nicked at least we can hold our heads up that we had a last go, the last fling and he goes fucking right and what's he do?' Danny made a raspberry noise to imitate an explosive bowel sound, highlighting Carl's unfortunate digestive condition.

'Well, that's what Brian said,' added Kenny, always seizing the opportunity to quote his favourite authority. 'I had problems and all.'

Danny didn't want to hear about Brian's woes. 'Fucking problems.'

Picking up on his antagonism, Kenny knew Danny

well enough to quickly backtrack. 'Well, we all got fucking problems.'

Terry was weary. 'Ken, I had problems. That's why I stayed.'

Kenny was sympathetic. They all knew Terry's money worries of old. 'More problems than the lot of us,' he nodded rapidly.

Terry was reflective. He was thinking back to the fateful second night again. 'That's why I stayed. I never thought I wouldn't stay.'

Danny wanted to let Terry know he appreciated the risk, his friend's bravery in going back. 'Well, you said, oh, we would get nicked and that. That's what you said.'

Whatever Danny and Terry have said about Carl, the truth is that they know he just found the whole thing exhausting. He was completely unable to cope with another night like the first one. It was 'past his bedtime'. The remaining men were in a frazzled mental state, but somehow needed to marshal all their finite, elderly reserves of strength to carry on.

CHAPTER SIX
THE BIG WIN

*'It was full of fucking bracelets and necklaces, full of them.
I said fucking hell…'* (Danny Jones)

The pace stepped up now, fuelled by adrenalin. Terry stayed the other side of the hole and passed through some vital kit to Danny and Basil who were in the vault. They used 'bolster' chisels to open the boxes. Their rough estimate was five to eight minutes to open each of the boxes. I estimate they would have been in there between two and a half and three and a half hours opening the boxes. The lock on the front of each box is very similar to a Yale lock, very simple. But it still takes time and effort to open them.

The police insist that the selection of boxes they opened was random. Danny and Terry, both officially and unofficially, very much indicate the same. The whole process at this point put me in mind of the broader changing face of crime in the UK's capital: a combination of extreme cunning with random serendipity.

One of the most fascinating aspects of researching this book has been to sit and talk to criminals and police officers about the nature of crime today. As one senior police officer said to me, it's much easier these days to defraud someone or launder money than hold up a Post Office van at gunpoint or try and break into a safe deposit. Our Hatton Garden guys really did take the harder path with their drilling, crawling and ransacking, and then the headache of hiding and selling on the loot piece by piece. Most modern criminals have simply moved on from this sort of risky, low-tech, old-fashioned robbery. Crime has changed and fraud is the fastest growing crime in the UK. We're being scammed like never before and fraud is the modern face of crime.

In 2016, fraud and cybercrime cost individuals, businesses, charities and the public sector £193 billion. These offences now account for close to half of all crime committed in Britain. Each of us is much more likely to be a victim of fraud than any other type of crime. These are crimes that can cause real heartache. Criminals often prey on the most vulnerable; exploiting the elderly, the lonely, those looking for love and those putting their trust and goodwill in faceless companies as well as small businesses who get targeted for money laundering. Less than half of all victims get their money back, and being a victim of fraud makes you even more likely to be targeted again – with con artists creating 'sucker lists' of people who've fallen for scams before.

The true scale of criminal fraud in Britain is far higher than previously thought because 85 per cent of fraud and cybercrime goes unreported, with victims either feeling embarrassed or believing that little can be done to catch the criminals responsible. Some of the latest figures from the City of London Police estimate that around 1.2 million crimes weren't reported by individuals and businesses in 2013–14, amounting to a cost of more than £12 billion.

In terms of their part in this bigger crime story, Danny and Terry had a chat on the afternoon of 15 May 2015, the first chat the police picked up on, when it is clear that the loot grab was very random.

Terry kicked things off: 'I wound up with none.'

Danny agreed, saying: 'You wound up with none, few little packets.'

Danny carried on: 'Fuck me, there's a lot of rings there, Tel.'

Terry nodded, cutting right to the chase. 'Sellable.'

Danny guessed that what they had was worth 'four or five grand or something like that.'

'We could chop all,' Terry offered.

Danny agreed. 'Yeah, chop all that.'

The 'chopping' that Danny and Terry are talking about here is how they divide up the loot to everyone's satisfaction. As part of the 'chop' Danny and Terry, particularly Terry, did not want to let anything go to waste. Baffled as they were in their attempts to assess the value of some of the more random items, they weren't going to discard them once other gang members and buyers had turned them down.

As Terry went on: 'All the shit they don't want we will have.'

Danny vehemently agreed. 'Yeah, that's it.'

So, although one convenient theory goes that if they knew so much about the alarms they may have known what boxes were worth opening, Danny and Terry don't really back this up.

The gang remember everyone's raised voices and excitement as they opened one box after another. Inside, joyous shouts accompanied the discovery of treasure: gold, silver and platinum bullion, jewellery, cash, foreign currency and – in packet after packet – loose diamonds. Even so, it was dirty, tiring, physically demanding labour. Excitement around the box opening was partly an attempt by Danny and Terry to elevate morale.

Danny was eagerly rifling through the loot now while Basil looked on.

Danny was yelling out his on-the-spot evaluations of some of the gear they were prising out of boxes: 'Sellable yes, necklaces all stone ones, few of them. Few of those bracelet ones, then you got this necklace with the fucking big emeralds in it with the matching earrings.' He waved it towards Terry.

'Another one there, they look nice… put stones in the necklace. Must be a couple hundred rings there, but he's got a wrap like that, two of them, full of rings and… big diamond rings there.'

Basil glanced up with a rare smile. Even 'wraps', relatively little packages of loot, could set them up very nicely in this enormously lucrative haul.

As more and more boxes were forced open, the loot

was passed through to Terry on the other side of the vault wall. Terry was in charge of sifting the contents and putting the booty inside the two wheelie bins they had brought with them. There was some kind of rudimentary system in place whereby stuff that obviously looked lower in value was tossed aside.

Danny and Terry weren't jewellery experts. Sometimes they were completely unsure what they were dealing with.

Danny tried to describe the necklaces: 'Them sort of funny stones in with one, each stone. Aquamarine they are called or something?'

'Yeah, yeah,' Terry agreed hastily.

'Won't make a dollar,' Danny assured baldly. 'But what we do is I'll look to see what the carat of the chain is and scarp them.'

Terry was equally at sea. 'Yeah, but just hope it ain't in silver, because normally if it's a shit stone, it's like a dress thing, isn't it?'

There is something rather endearing about these old geezers floundering over their attempts to understand and value women's finery.

Danny was unusually hesitant. 'I don't think they'd make that in silver, the work that's gone into the…'

'No, I know,' said Terry.

Danny was able to demonstrate some self-awareness. 'Do you know what I mean, I could be wrong. I hope I'm wrong!'

'No!' Terry said reassuringly.

'I've been wrong many times,' Danny said wearily.

On this basis, sorting the boxes effectively, under conditions of crazy pressure, was an uphill climb.

Two gang associates close to Danny have told me that as soon as he got in, Basil went over to one numbered box, broke it open and took one specific thing. Only then did Basil join Danny jimmying open the rest of the boxes. However, I don't believe this to be true. In any case, they opened dozens of safe deposit boxes, which they proceeded to ransack.

But by 5am only 73 of the 999 boxes in the vault had been opened. Much to the men's chagrin, a crushingly disappointing 29 of the boxes were empty, with rent not paid on them. Forcing each box open one by one was a gruelling and exhausting job, and it was gutting when, after all that, the damn box was empty.

Of course, some also contained the kind of high-value items they had really gone to all this bother for. There was paperwork scattered everywhere and the contents of the boxes all jumbled together in some cases. It was time to start clearing out. It was instinct, honed over decades, which told them this. I reckon it was also Basil's access to something of use – Carlos's visitor diary, a tip-off that Lionel Wiffen's electrician was going to pay a visit soon. There was a practical point too – the wheelie bins were full to the brim with booty.

CHAPTER SEVEN
THE ESCAPE

'In our world you either stay or you go.'
(Danny Jones)

Instinctively, after all that effort, Terry and Danny would have taken more, given more time. They could have brought in a third wheelie bin for their second visit. They could have kitted themselves out more effectively. They were angered at Brian and Carl for the fact they were two sets of hands down.

At just after 5am, Danny had the presence of mind to deal with some of the forensics, as they had the first time they left the vault. He used a special spray to get rid of any traces of DNA. He thoroughly rinsed down all the tools with bleach. The men cleared most of their tools from the vault… but not all of them.

They left behind the big drill bits used to bore the hole and, absolutely critically for the subsequent investigation, bits of the broken hydraulic pump from the first night – still attached to the acrow prop.

Basil went to Kenny's look-out point, roused him once more, and told him that it was time to get back in the van.

CCTV footage at 5.45am recorded Danny on the stairs carrying the Clarke pump. He went back inside and then Terry and Danny brought the wheelie bins up the stairs.

This was a mammoth and unpleasant task because of how incredibly heavy the full bins were. Not for the first time that evening, Danny wondered if Terry was going to make it. Shattered, and gasping for breath, Terry toiled on tortuously with the bins.

They put everything next to the metal fire door exit. Basil carefully locked the fire exit door to the courtyard, sliding the two bolts across from inside exactly as he had done before. Like the first time, depending on whether Basil had the key to the door to the stairs that run from basement to the ground floor foyer, he either used the stairs or he climbed up the lift shaft. Kenny collected the van. Basil left through the 88–90 front entrance.

CCTV captured some more interesting details here. Kenny drove up to the metal fire door exit. Terry and Danny moved everything onto the street. Basil walked calmly down Greville Street. He was still, of course, meticulously carrying the black bin liner to guard him from the gaze of the CCTV cameras. Basil helped the men to load everything inside the van.

At 6.45am on the Sunday, after a hell of a night, an exhausted Danny, Terry and Basil got into the white Transit van driven by Kenny. It pulled away along Greville Street. With a combined age of 448, they had been up all night for two separate nights over one long weekend. Pumping with stress and adrenalin, they now wanted to collapse. CCTV footage subsequently recorded the white van arriving at Kenny Collins' house in Bletsoe Walk, Islington, again.

Although I know that the all-important divvy-up was firmly scheduled for the next day, what we don't know is where the wheelie bins and bags were stored on this crucial first day. Danny and Terry never revealed that. Were all the wheelie bins and bags unloaded and stored in Kenny's house, or was all the loot stored somewhere else nearby? I'm told they were either stored at Kenny's or round the back 'in plain sight', but there may be some smoke and mirrors operating here.

What was Basil doing and saying regarding his share of the treasure? He doesn't miss a trick and would have been very carefully monitoring any operation to store the loot. Maybe Basil slept at Kenny's house the night before the divvy-up, to physically keep watch? Did Danny take everything, not just the jewellery we know that he made off with and hid in the graveyard?

It seems like the gang decided to put their trust in Kenny to look after all the gear, despite the likelihood he would be unable to resist taking a dip, because they simply had no other choice. The brief interlude between the van arriving and leaving – just a quarter of an hour – strongly suggests that the bins were taken inside the Bletsoe house. It also indicates to me that they didn't have much time for any clever business like sealing the bins and bags so it would be clear if anyone had tampered with them.

Cropley Street CCTV captured the white van leaving. As he was driving Terry away, Danny was asking Terry if they were sure they could trust Kenny with all the gear left at Bletsoe Walk.

Terry didn't have a really satisfying answer for him. 'We have no choice in the matter, Dan.'

Meanwhile, Lionel Wiffen was back on Greville Street preparing to let the electrician in. At that point Lionel noticed that the door was unlocked and ajar again. Just as the door was unlocked and ajar again, so Lionel followed the same drill: a cautious inspection for signs of a break-in followed by reassurance once nothing seemed out of place on the surface and the basement door was still locked.

At 8am, Danny drove Terry to a scrapyard. Did they pay to have the van, a critical piece of evidence, crushed there? Did they use the locale to transfer the bins to Danny's Land Rover if they had not been left at Bletsoe Walk?

This slightly odd 24-hour wait for the divvy-up was hugely tense. They had come so far but not got their hands on the goods yet. There were so many variables at play. Could Kenny be trusted? What was Basil's angle on all this – he had seemed much more focused and process-driven regarding what he wanted to get out of the vault? Was Brian Reader going to make a reappearance and demand, or help himself to, his share? Danny and Terry, and probably Basil too, were also sorely tempted to go back for a third attempt to get more than 73 boxes opened out of nearly 1,000.

The door that was left open might yield some interesting insights into whether they intended to go back for a third time. After all, on the second night when they got back in, they left the back door open again. Was this just an oversight, or did it signal the intention to go in for a further attempt to get more of the boxes' contents?

Why didn't they close it once they were done the second time? Were they considering going back in a third time? Or is there perhaps a feature of that back door that means you have to have a key to close it properly so they couldn't shut it?

One of my best sources on the escape replied, 'I doubt they were going back again as it was getting close to the end of the bank holidays, and they only went back as they had problems with the tools for the vault.'

What was unequivocally clear is that the absence of a plan after the job meant that a series of problems began to surface. These included, but were certainly not limited to:

1. The vehicles they used. The white Transit van was stuffed with the two wheelie bins full

of jewels and two canvas holdalls. And they didn't know exactly where they were going to put it all. The other vehicle, a distinctive white Mercedes E200, with alloy rims and a black roof, was also a problem. This was the car they had used to return to Hatton Garden *and* to rush to Twickenham to buy the new and improved replacement pump in Val Jones's name. This rookie error would come back to haunt them.

2. Brian Reader. He might have walked away from the raid, but he sure as hell wasn't going to walk away from his share of the haul. Was he going to inveigle his way back into the gang to get his share of the loot via manipulating Billy 'The Fish', or could he use Basil as the conduit to get him back to the precious loot? Brian's departure had caused other problems, too. The gang didn't anticipate having to shift the loot with Brian out of the picture. Brian knew the most about valuing the gear and who to sell it to. When Brian walked off the job, the other gang members (except Carl and possibly Basil) were shocked and furious. Danny and Terry stepped up in a hurry and didn't have the chance to think it all through properly and

come up with a new plan now that Brian was not involved.

In reality, everyone was trying to grab their share, and there was frequent disagreement about what that share might be. As one gang member told me, 'Everyone was trying to take a "dip". No one could trust anyone. We were panicking, really.'

On that basis, who exactly were they going to trust with the haul? Although Danny and Terry seem to have assumed that Kenny Collins was always going to end up storing the stolen property, they admit that they hadn't thought through, in any real, structured way, how he was going to do it. He just was. Danny and Terry slightly misjudged Kenny's abilities on this critical point. They reckoned he would be able to sort it himself without dragging anyone else, potentially someone compromising, into it with him. But it turns out he wasn't capable of that…

Danny says, 'The reason that it all fell apart was the lack of a proper after-plan. The "doing" was impressive. The after-plan was a disaster.'

Another anonymous source very close to the crime

has elaborated on this for us and has their own ideas. They told me: 'The order of it falling apart was soft Kenny being listened to. He led the police to Brian who led to Terry who led to Danny. And Basil is the only one who got away. The only one never to show his face and the only one to use a fake name.'

After the escape and before the divvy-up, Danny in particular was keeping a close eye on the news, waiting for the robbery story to break. The discovery could only be a matter of hours away, and then it was just down to the Met making it public. They'd had various unwelcome punters crawling all over the premises even over the bank holiday weekend anyway. One of them was bound to be about to discover the almighty mess that the gang had left.

Even at this point, though, Danny and Terry were thinking through their options of who to sell to, naturally including their key buyer, 'Frank'. Throughout early 2015 the pair had also been casually scouting out other potential venues to offload the jewels without their owners' knowledge.

What was everybody else up to at this point? Well, Billy Lincoln decided to take a break in the sun. He flew out to Rhodes and then caught a ferry to the unspoiled little Greek paradise island of Symi, spending a relaxing fortnight away.

Danny also booked a trip, giving the search for buyers a rest for a few days. He needed to get away, so he went to Crete for a week with Val's brother and sister-in-law. Val is terrified of flying so she didn't go.

Terry was rather cynical about holidays, noting that, 'Yeah when you get the Sunday papers about a third of the paper is holidays. Mind you, I've noticed after Christmas is over, they start advertising holidays.'

'They are fucking relentless, aren't they,' agreed Danny.

Terry wryly observed, 'If you had to work for a living, you know an ordinary job not a good job, how you managed to get by Christmas and then start fucking take the kids on holiday. Fucking hell.'

When Danny got back from his little break, Terry told Danny everything that had been happening. They had no idea that they were being recorded, or of the media frenzy that would ensue once the ransacked vault was opened.

This is all part of a broader story about the changing landscape of London crime, too. Since the early 1990s, 'true crime' has become big business in the UK. Vintage true crime, featuring old-school details like what was playing on the jukebox in the Blind Beggar pub in East London when Ron Kray shot George Cornell in 1966, is the kind of fascinating detail we are all susceptible to. From the very beginning I had seen that the Hatton Garden heist members were part of this tradition. Today's organised crime is more mundane. It's largely all about trading relationships, capitalism, internet fraud and money laundering through car washes and hair salons.

This is pretty much my experience of talking to villains. It is simply what they do and they take it seriously and move cautiously. And they talk to very few people. I think this is why we want to glamourise it so much: to fill in the gaps, to add colour when they say so little to outsiders. Take our guys on this job. All their police interviews and many of their trial statements were: 'No comment'. Later, they pleaded guilty in the face of overwhelming evidence, said almost nothing in court and hardly talked to anyone, even in Belmarsh. So all the journalists had to fill in the gaps and add the colour to make for a good story.

Dick Hobbs, emeritus professor of sociology at the University of Essex and a specialist on organised and professional crime in London, says that the biggest misconception about his field of study is that organised crime is a terrain populated exclusively by 'characters'. He sees it as a cocktail of *The Godfather*, *The Wire* and *Only Fools and Horses* mixed by Guy Ritchie. This is where I part company from him a little. As, although I know what he means, I have found in my experience of researching for this book that serious villains *are* often fantastic characters. Well dressed and charming, and generous in their own way, carrying their wedges of £50 notes, but utterly amoral. And there is something beguiling and fascinating about them. Because they don't work in regular mundane jobs they have more time than the rest of us to sit around and shoot the breeze. And as a result, they are often quick-witted and amusing, used to hours and hours of banter and chat while eating and drinking and being out and about. There is a certain amount of bragging to sit through, but there was plenty of witty banter between our gang too.

Of course, it's unlikely that Carl saw the funny side of an exchange between Danny, Terry and Kenny.

Danny observed that Carl copied Brian, and Terry responded by calling Carl, 'an arsehole'.

Danny went one further of the incontinent Carl, saying, 'Carl's arsehole fell out.'

Kenny as usual was inclined to spring to Brian's

defence a bit and contrast his walking off the job with Carl's decision: 'Carl's different – his arsehole went. His [Brian's] arsehole never went – he thought we'd never get in.'

Danny was enjoying this exchange. 'No, that's right – he thought we would never get in and Carl's arsehole went.'

Kenny was warming to the theme, too. 'His arsehole went and he thought we would never get in, cause even that cunt, I said give it another half hour, fuck we've done everything we can do, if we can't get in, we won't be able to get in, will we.'

This exchange caused consternation when part of it was read out in court. For the case to come to court though, the crime had to be discovered in the first place.

CHAPTER EIGHT

THE DISCOVERY

'It is empty, we have to live with that. There is absolutely nothing you can do about it.' (Kjeld Jacobsen, Hatton Garden heist victim and retired jeweller)

On the morning of Tuesday, 7 April the world was about to discover just how eventful this particular bank holiday had been. After being tipped off by a colleague, Kelvin Stockwell called the police to say that there had been a break-in. At 8am, he entered the premises and started to spot that things were not as they should be.

He spoke at the trial about exactly what he discovered.

Stockwell said: 'I looked and there was a lock on the door and that had been popped, there was a hole through the wall and I saw that we had been burgled… On the floor there was drills, cutting material, the lights were on and the second floor (lift) barriers were left open. I went into the yard to get a signal and dialled 999.'

Stockwell, with two decades of service at Hatton Garden under his belt, along with fellow security guard Keefer Kamara, with 12 years' experience, and the Building Manager Carlos Cruse, all have a really important part to play in filling the blanks that the robbers aren't willing to fill at this point in the story. They have given a very helpful combination of verbal accounts, witness statements and trial evidence.

The emergency call led to local Metropolitan Police officers arriving to seal off the area. The first policeman at the scene from the Metropolitan Police's Flying Squad, the branch in charge of investigating commercial robberies, was DC Jamie Day, and he was to become a key player in this story.

Day found dust and paperwork everywhere. He discovered that the water feed required by the drill had been very inefficiently and messily fed by the robbers from a bucket straight into the drill. The bucket was set precariously on top of one of the green recycled crates that the perpetrators had brought in with them.

Totally backing up what the gang have told me, the opening and sorting of the boxes themselves seemed opportunistic and chaotic. Some safe-deposit box holders' valuables had got knocked into other people's boxes in the frantic attempt to sort the wheat from the chaff as quickly as possible. There was no system.

In terms of how they got in, although technically only members can enter the vault after filling out an entry book note, Kelvin Stockwell did admit he had let four or five prospective customers in the year before the raid to have a nose around the vault with no record kept. Lionel Wiffen told the police that the Greville Street door was left ajar.

Police forensics was soon well underway, but they also needed to attend to the critical task of collecting CCTV footage from all the shops around the vicinity of the crime. It was painstaking stuff. The police had to work across 120 sites, many of them with several CCTV cameras each. The police ended up working on it for an entire week.

Coming back to the end of the first day of investigation, the key police officers – DCI Paul Johnson, DC Jamie Day and Detective Superintendent

Craig Turner – met up to perform a formal situation report. At that stage, they clung firmly onto the hope that a combination of hard-core forensics and trawling through endless CCTV footage was going to lead them to the perpetrators sooner rather than later.

The robbery was certainly not viewed by the police as a victimless crime. It didn't take much time for Hatton Garden depositors to start coming forward describing what they had lost. Many of them, much to their chagrin looking at it with 20/20 hindsight, were not insured.

In a piece for *The Telegraph*, features writer Joe Shute detailed the losses of some people he had interviewed, including a 47-year-old trader called Hussein Batcha. 'Batcha was one of many people still waiting to find out what has happened to the contents of his security box, rented for a few hundred pounds a year. Batcha said, "Some of the people will easily have lost half a million from what they had in there. Most of us don't have insurance; we never thought we would be in this position."'

'Jerry Landon, a Hatton Garden trader for nearly 50 years, also spent an anxious week. The 77-year-old recently put items of jewellery worth "hundreds of thousands" into two boxes in the security deposit, because he was due to go into hospital for a knee operation and would be out of action for seven weeks. "I still haven't heard anything," he said yesterday, "the whole situation is very distressing."

Shute continues: 'Tony Dellow is another proud old-timer, having been based in Hatton Garden since 1976. His jewellery workshop is situated past two security doors on the second-floor of a brick building opposite 88–90. He stands proudly next to a huge safe painted in the colours of West Ham Football Club. He has not been affected by the raid, but admits it has "devastated" the street.'

Along with the media hungry for more information on this extraordinary crime, the depositors were clamouring for information from the police – information the police couldn't, or wouldn't, dish out just yet.

Retired jeweller Kjeld Jacobsen told Margaret Davis in a story published by the *Mirror* on 14 January 2016 what would become a pretty familiar story among the depositors. After 45 years as a jeweller, he set aside what was meant to be the bulk of his pension and stashed it in a box at the Hatton Garden Safe Deposit Company. The police told him the morning after the heist that his box was among those raided. He called his wife and told her, 'It is empty, we have to live with that. There is absolutely nothing you can do about it.'

The point he added was critical in terms of this case: 'I could have insured it with ease and it wouldn't have been expensive, but you don't normally insure when you put things into a safe-deposit box.' The testimony of such depositors was to prove critical later, because they had no agenda in exaggerating what had gone missing from their safe deposit boxes. Sadly for them, there was no insurance claim to be made or exaggerated.

Further down the line, when the case came to court, gang member Hugh Doyle had a somewhat sanctimonious attitude to the depositors' plight, probably fuelled by the rude things that Danny and Terry were revealed to have been saying about him: Outside court, he told *The Telegraph*: 'I'm happy and relieved, I just need to catch my breath. I feel sorry for the victims. Now I'm going to focus on my business and my family.'

Soon after the spectacular story broke, the media began to speculate about the identities of the bold robbers, much to the amusement of the Hatton Garden gang. As one gang member put it to me: 'Fuck, they couldn't have been more wrong in some cases, could they? Eastern European gangsters?'

Obviously rather fired up to get his moment in the sun, speaking to *The Guardian* on 10 April 2015 was Jason Coghlan, a reformed armed robber who now owns and operates a Malaga-based business which represents Brits who have been charged with crimes in Spain and Thailand. His speculation was comically inaccurate:

'I would not be surprised if the men behind the raid were from Eastern Europe because that's where all of the best thieves come from these days,' he said. 'I would be equally unsurprised to find out that the loot had very quickly found its way out of the United Kingdom and into Europe for disbursement to more friendly places to wash such hot gems and cash, which is very likely to be reinvested into the narcotics industry, because that provides a pension for villains to live comfortably off for life, rather than a potential headache hidden some place that it might be discovered.'

The papers were way off in some of their speculation about how the robbers entered the building too. On 26 April 2015, reporter Declan Lawn ran a long piece for the BBC in which he tried to mimic the break-in himself, coming to the conclusion that it was difficult if not impossible.

'It's still unclear as to how exactly the thieves got into the building. They may have had someone inside the building simply waiting for the last person to leave, or could have gained access from adjoining rooftops. One day last week – while the police investigation unfolded downstairs – I managed to talk my way in to the access laneway at the side of the building, the very place where the thieves were captured on CCTV. If I could manage blagging access in 10 minutes flat, imagine what an organised gang could do over several months.'

Needless to say, Danny found this kind of wild speculation completely hilarious.

At this point in the story, it is hard to believe but important to remember that initially the press had no clue about who, how or when regarding the Hatton Garden heist. Major papers were using absurd diagrams showing a gang cutting through the roof before tunnelling their way through two thick walls just to get into the building's lift shaft. Many news outlets were (utterly wrongly) convinced that they used ropes to abseil down the shaft into the basement, smashed their way through a false wall and finally, as their pièce de résistance, cut through an 18-inch-thick metal door into the vault itself!

THE DISCOVERY

However, it didn't take long for the media to latch onto one of the most enduring and appealing aspects of the case – the idea of the 'ordinary decent criminal', which Danny Jones and Terry Perkins encapsulate pretty much as neatly as anyone can.

Speaking to *The Guardian* a few days after the heist, a couple of anonymous criminals unsurprisingly had much better instincts regarding how it had happened and what would happen next than most other people.

'One former armed robber from south London has his own theory as to why the theft has attracted such attention and speculation. "It's gone back to the old days, hasn't it?" he said. "No one's been injured. No one's been shot. Everybody's happy because everybody's skint at the moment and they reckon – rightly or wrongly – that whoever's lost something can afford it.

"Who's done it? Well, whoever it is has got some very good inside information about the alarm not working and they've obviously done their homework. They knew the layout and they must have known that Hatton Garden is full of CCTV cameras so they'll have all been in disguise. Maybe they have military training but only certain people would have the balls – the audacity – to pull off something like that."

'Another former robber said the stolen goods would already be at their destination. "This is no bunch of mugs. They're never going to be nicking this stuff without it having a place to go to already arranged." As for getting it out of the country these days: "It's a doddle. The same people who import drugs and weapons into Britain will be able to take anything out in the other direction. It won't be in a box in the back of a van, it'll be mixed up with something like a furniture assignment and I'd be surprised if it's not out of Britain already. And it will have all been split up, they won't have all their eggs in one basket.'

Joe Shute, writing in *The Telegraph* on 10 April 2015, was pursuing a different, very interesting line of inquiry, one which even today is still unresolved, but which I return to in detail towards the end of this book. Was there an inside man? Grizzled former policemen were happy to share their views with me. Barry Phillips, a retired detective chief superintendent and a former member of the Metropolitan Police Flying Squad had this to say: 'What [the gang] have overcome to get into the vault is unbelievable... That takes a great degree of insider knowledge, expertise and ability to call on the experts who can breach the security arrangements. There are less than a handful of individuals who have got the wherewithal to be able to get the insider information and have the contacts and financial clout to put this job together.'

Shute, in the same piece, also eloquently captured the public fascination with how this impregnable vault had been breached. Once it was discovered the breach was achieved by a few frail old men, the story became explosive... 'The raid is regarded as an incredible feat not least because the basement vault was deemed the safest place in London's jewellery quarter, used both by members of the public and the traders who work in the area to store their stock. And also of course by the shady characters long associated with this part of the capital, an area that still harks back to a seedier age, as a way of keeping criminal proceeds away from prying eyes. The vault is normally only accessible through three doors; the first barred like a prison cell, the last made of metal, 18 inches thick. And if the guards at any point along the route don't recognise your face, they won't let you pass. On Diamond Street where everything rests on reputation, the Deposit was presumed impregnable.'

One aspect of the break-in which had helped the gang beyond measure – the police failing to respond to the alarm going off – was now being used as a stick to beat the police with, and this was massively getting their backs up. Danny believes this is when the police started to really 'get it in' for the gang and hope to make an example of them. The thieves had mugged off the police.

As CNN reported on 10 April 2015: 'British police investigating a spectacular heist in the heart of London's jewellery district said they knew a burglar alarm went off but didn't respond. Southern Monitoring Alarm Company called (the police) at 12:21a.m. April 3 to report that the burglar alarm had been activated at Hatton Garden Safe Deposit Ltd., MPS said in a prepared statement.

"The call was recorded and transferred to the police's CAD (computer-aided dispatch) system. A grade was applied to the call that meant that no police response was deemed to be required. We are now investigating why this grade was applied to the call. This investigation is being carried out locally. It is too early to say if the handling of the call would have had an impact on the outcome of the incident."'

The negative PR made the police feel the need to make an additional statement from outside the scene of the crime. Flying Squad DCI Paul Johnson announced that 'There were no signs of a forced entry. The thieves have disabled the communal lift on the second floor and then used the lift shaft to climb down into the basement. Once inside they forced open up to seventy safety deposit boxes. The scene is chaotic. The vault is covered in dust and debris and the floor is strewn with discarded safety deposit boxes and power tools, including an angle grinder, concrete drills and crowbars. It's a sophisticated offence clearly and would take some pre-planning. The people who planned it knew how they were going to go about it. I imagine that pool of people is quite limited. Whether that involves some inside knowledge will form part of the investigation.'

The police also went public with a picture of the hole cut in the wall. This was where the story exploded even further. There was widespread, utter disbelief that anyone could fit through that hole. Was the person that did a contortionist, a child, a magician? I couldn't help but smile as I read through all the early press cuttings while I was researching the book.

CHAPTER NINE

THE LOOT

*'We are doing what we should have done and
what I said. Gone to his house, bag it up, and go to that
flat of mine and stay there for a week.'* (Terry)

I was told by the gang that on Sunday 5 April, they
had travelled to Kenny's house at Bletsoe Walk in
Islington with all the gear stuffed into wheelie bins. I
wanted, of course, to know exactly where the bins had
come from. After the job, Val said her sister came over
and said, 'Someone's nicked me bins!!!'. It turned out
that it was Danny, who had taken Val's sister's bins off

the drive as a way to transport the loot from the vault and for the divvy-up.

Extraordinarily, they didn't take the bins into the house. They were, in fact, hidden in plain sight around the side and back of the property – after a thorough check that the following morning was not bin collection day. The van was then efficiently disposed of through their extended contact network of garage owners, mechanics and car dealers.

The following morning, gang members made a series of very quick phone calls: Danny called Terry, Kenny called Terry, and Billy called Kenny, basically all to arrange meeting up at Kenny's, although Terry and Danny met up at Danny's first. Terry cautioned during these calls that other criminals were going to be nosing around the loot and 'needed to be kept the fuck out of it'. About 9.30am, Terry and Danny met back at Kenny's house and the divvy-up started, which lasted most of the day.

Unbelievably, and I think this is my favourite detail in the entire case, the gear in the wheelie bins and holdalls was split with a toss of a coin. They grabbed stuff out of the wheelie bins and if more than one person wanted the same thing they would toss a coin to see who got it.

THE LOOT

As they said to me with a simple shrug, 'That's the way we have always done it in the past on other jobs. And this one was no different.'

I find it a beautifully simple, utterly captivating, logical and childlike way to split stolen treasure.

As part of my research, I've had many meetings with one villain who wasn't involved in Hatton Garden but who has been involved in jobs like this before, albeit on a smaller scale. He told me that they made a schoolboy error in the divvy-up. 'You need to divide up the stuff man by man. One takes care of the watches, another one the gold bars, another the diamonds and precious stones, another the cash and so on and so on. You don't just lay it all out on the floor, do a dip and leave it to chance. It's too messy and that's where the arguments come in about who has what.'

Hindsight is a wonderful thing though. The coin toss was not only as old school as it gets, but also a representation in microcosm of just how amateurish and seat-of-the-pants the divvy-up really was.

In the recorded conversations between the gang members, there was disquiet in the Danny/Terry camp about aspects of the divvy-up. Danny was very mistrustful of Kenny, who could be sharp when he wanted to be, and he took loot very seriously. As the divvy-up got underway in Kenny's living room, Danny said to Terry, 'Remember, watch him. He wants it all his own way. Does it all clever you know, I'll tell you.'

'Yeah.' Terry was in agreement.

Not only that, but Kenny was also, in the two men's eyes, capable of throwing the baby out with the bathwater. Terry had to rescue some of the loot from Kenny's carelessness, as he described: 'All that shit he's going to throw away, I put it all in the bag – we'll have that!'

'Oh yeah!' exclaimed Danny.

'And we can decide whether it's shit or not!' Terry pointed out.

'Yeah, of course.' Danny was in perfect harmony with his old chum. 'Like all those fucking stones I got.'

Terry agreed. 'I think the watches we got… well, I don't know the make of them.'

'Ohhh…' Danny wasn't able to offer much help. And as for Kenny…

'We probably had the wrong parcels,' griped Terry. 'He's got the fucking parcel.'

Terry knew why slip-ups were being made in the divvy-up. 'Too much of a hurry up, it was… Do you know what I mean, you don't do that, you sort out your parcels and say what's left, you give him that.

That is not the way to do things,' Terry concluded firmly.

'No,' Danny quietly agreed.

Terry had a bee squarely in his bonnet. 'You don't know what you're getting, you don't know what's there, you don't.'

There is a sense, particularly via Terry, that Kenny rather enjoyed the glamour associated with the criminal fraternity linking him to the robbery and bigging it up a bit. However, Terry was certainly relying on Kenny to play a role in the storing and disposing of stolen jewellery, and to deal with the less high-worth items.

It was Kenny and, critically, Brian's contacts who would be the buyers. This network is what enabled Brian to get back into the frame. That said, Brian does not appear to have been part of the divvy-up, so it is important not to, as most other narratives have done, exaggerate Brian's full return to the gang. He wasn't brought in as the Guv'nor, or on the exact same footing as before.

One gang member told me that it had been Brian's suggestion for Billy to look after bags of loot that hadn't yet been divvyed-up. And several gang associates including Arthur have made it clear to me that there was a very low level of comfort about the quantity of loot – much of which the rest of the gang hadn't even looked at – that got left with Billy. Another gang member told me that Terry went to Kenny's house furious that Brian had hatched a plan with Billy to have a dip in the loot together. It was all a cunning plan for Brian to get himself back in, he thought.

Terry described confronting Brian to Danny: 'I said to Brian, I said, ere, how does this fucking Bill know about anything? I said the fucking geezer round Kenny's. Brian said, "I went upstairs to have a shower, right, and when I came down there was a bloke there who I never knew, which was Bill and Kenny had told him everything." I said cos Bill has wound up with the fucking gear. He has given it to someone else to look after and all them big stones are already gone. I said that's what you fucking done. That's how you fucking left us.'

It's possible that Terry was overstating the aggression of his response to Brian for Danny's benefit and, once again, to big himself up in a pissing contest with the Guv'nor. Even so, this was clearly a very frank and heated exchange between Terry and Brian, with Brian denying any connection to Billy.

Danny also suspected someone had already had a dip and tried to tally up working forwards from his own stash: 'Well I've got my own gear, that's it, I tell you what, he's got a heap of gear you know.'

Terry was taking the lead on the mental arithmetic this time. 'Well he's fucking got to have otherwise we got fucking 300 grand each.'

Danny was trying to fathom out the jewellery too. 'Well I'll tell you something and all – you don't realise what you got because there are hundreds and hundreds of rings, Tel, you know what I mean, there's loads of them.'

Also totting things up in his head, Terry carried on, 'Well I hope we get close to the mil, don't you?'

Danny agreed, 'Yes, so do I'.

Terry was marvelling, 'Fucking hell he's got to have a lot more gold then.'

Danny returned obsessively to his previous point about a certain someone taking more than his fair share and skimming some off before the divvy-up. 'He's got a heap of gear, Tel; play your cards right, he's got them first two bags…'

Of all the lingering mysteries and unanswered question I was working through in my examination of this unique case, the immediate aftermath of the divvy-up is the point that the gang have deliberately left most hazy.

The tension was certainly mounting. In fact, it was more than tension, it was downright ugly, not just around who had to store the goods but also around how they could be safely sold and who took the responsibility for all of that. It seems likely that the conflict during the divvy-up was sufficiently heightened for it to bring about some change to the plan, such as the 'plan' was. This may well have been, for instance, when Basil decided to skip the country, rather than it being more premeditated than that.

'Thieves and ponces,' spat Danny of his fellow gang members.

'And took people on, that's what they have done,' scowled Terry, on his pet subject of other people's indiscretion again.

'Thieves, ponces, don't take it, it's all laid there,' Danny fumed.

'I am beginning to fucking hate them, I am,' declared Terry.

'All fucking idiots,' said Danny succinctly.

'They are fucking idiots,' nodded Terry.

Danny was still pissed off with Brian. 'That Brian, he didn't half give me the hump then, I said stop being fucking silly. I said, when you are young you do the angle and buzz of it, I said not fucking there. See, cos he's got nothing to go to, he is just a horrible man.'

'He is fucked now,' Terry assured Danny.

'He is fucked,' Danny agreed.

'He's fucked. He can't tell us nothing.' Terry didn't have much time to spare for Brian, either.

Danny also wanted to make it clear that Brian wasn't getting, 'a penny out of me, not a fucking bit.'

'No, no Kenny will give him some money,' said Terry, gullible Kenny proving to be the butt of the jokes again.

'Kenny.' Danny injected maximum scorn into the word.

Terry had an altogether more benign destination in mind for his loot. 'Nothing he can tell me, fuck all, my little granddaughter's having it.'

'Yeah, that's right, your little grand daughter,' said Danny approvingly. Family first, after all. Just not Brian's family. 'Yeah fuck him, fuck his daughter, fuck his will, fuck Kenny, fuck them.'

Some very important new personalities start to enter the story in earnest at this point. It wasn't just about the men in the vault any more. And as more people got involved, the greater the chance there was of someone shooting their mouth off where they shouldn't. With all these people involved, someone was going to let something slip even if they thought they were being careful, vigilant and crafty.

Take Jon Harbinson, Billy Lincoln's nephew, a man in his early 40s and a taxi driver by trade. Given what Jon did for a living, Terry was mad-keen to get Jon involved so that he could anonymously transport the stolen property. A close associate of the gang told me about his uncle, who was responsible for some armed robberies back in the 1960s. They had two types of getaway car – one was a London taxi and the other, for central London robberies, a chauffeur-driven Bentley. In different environments both could melt into the background and slowly creep off after a job.

Six years older than Jon Harbinson, Enfield plumber Hugh Doyle was also getting involved.

But with the loot getting spread thinner, the circle of trust was loosening and getting cast perilously wider. Kenny wanted to know what was going to happen about Brian. Danny and Terry were equally unambiguous in their response: Brian could 'go fuck himself.'

A chat a month later between Danny and Terry made the corrosion of trust over the Brian issue with Kenny crystal clear.

Danny's opening remark on him was blunt: 'Ken, you only sat up in the fucking room and fell asleep.'

Terry nodded. 'I know.'

Danny continued of Kenny, 'You never done no graft...'

Terry's resentment over Kenny's indiscretion boiled over at this point. 'And told someone you shouldn't have! And Brian, I'll ask him if I get a chance, I'll say, how does that fucking Bill know?'

Danny responded fiercely. 'Cos of Brian, him and Brian.'

Terry shook his head impatiently. 'Asking him the cunt out in the open. You guarantee Kenny has told them all about it, every mortal thing.'

I get the sense that part of their anger towards Brian and the way they vented it in the recorded conversations was because they did need him to fence and sell on the loot.

Obviously it pissed them off that this was the case. After the disastrous first night, they didn't want to have to rely on him.

They couldn't literally 'take stock', because not one of them knew exactly what they had. Also, it seems that they barely knew the value of anything except the really obvious things like gold, diamonds and cash.

They didn't know when they filled the bins in the vaults and they didn't know when they were trying to work out if someone had taken a dip.

Terry warned Danny, 'You wouldn't know if someone's took a stone out of these parcels.'

'No, no.' Danny could see Terry's point.

Terry was once again warming to his theme. 'Would ya, wouldn't have a clue.'

'You'd never know in a million years,' agreed Danny.

'No.' Terry shook his head.

Danny was running his mental calculations again. 'You know he said to me about seven million, I don't know what ever it was, I'm thinking what was there…'

'What?' Terry wanted to know.

Danny kept calculating. 'I am thinking you know you said on the news there was…'

Terry butted in, remembering. 'a 12 stone…12 carat…12 carat diamond.'

'Yeah,' Danny jabbed his finger at Terry for emphasis.

Terry smiled. 'Yeah Frank [their key buyer] said, "Is it there?" I said "I ain't got no fucking clue."'

'I ain't seen that,' added Danny.

Clearly thinking again about someone taking a dip,

Terry carried on, 'That's what I am afraid, that either Bill or someone's going "That's for me".'

It's not known when Danny and Terry left the divvy-up in the Land Rover, partly because they have deliberately concealed whether Basil was with them or if he had already vanished after taking his share. Was he at a key UK exit point already? Dover, Heathrow, Gatwick, Folkestone, Southend? And was Danny up at the cemetery shortly afterwards burying jewels?

Automatic number plate recognition helpfully indicates that Billy's Audi was on City Road. Then there is evidence of Billy at Bletsoe Walk before calling Jon, Danny and Terry in his Black Land Rover on the A10 heading for Enfield. Next Jon was sighted at Billy's house in Bethnal Green, picking up the three holdalls.

I do know that Terry went back home. Terry stashed his share under some floorboards and behind a length of skirting board. Then it was time for another of his thrice-daily insulin injections. Terry was a tough guy who had led a tough life, but he was being tested to the limit by this experience, physically and emotionally.

Kenny took his dog for a drive in his Mercedes. Thanks to his health issues and long-term fitness aversion, Kenny doesn't like walking, but he wanted some fresh air and the dog needed to do its business.

Kenny just drove to a scrubby area of open ground, opened the door, and let the dog out for some spring weather.

On 15 May 2015, Danny and Terry were making plans to link up with each other and then for Kenny to deal with some of the gear.

Danny assured Terry, 'Monday night I'll come down and see you where all the cars are.'

Terry was amenable, but wanted to know, 'Will it go in my boot?'

'Yeah,' said Danny.

In that case, Terry agreed, 'I'll meet you and just sling it in the boot.'

Terry remembered an issue with taking his daughter to the airport on Sunday night.

'Yeah, what time?' Danny wanted to know.

'I got to find out,' explained Terry.

'I could be back Monday at 12 o'clock?' Danny offered.

'Yeah, yeah,' Terry said, fine with that plan.

'I could get to my brother's, leave at 9,' reasoned Danny.

Terry grimaced as he remembered Kenny suddenly. 'Oh, we got to go and see that cunt.'

'Oh yeah.' Danny was grimacing too.

THE LOOT

The two men agreed that they could do it in the evening.

'Yeah, I forgot that,' acknowledged Terry. 'He said I'll see you Tuesday – where is he going to see us? That's how much he thinks, where is he going to see us? I thought he said I'd see you Tuesday, he is bringing it over.'

Danny's tone was slightly irascible, as it usually was when thinking of Kenny. 'I'm gonna say, "Ken look, what's happening with that gear is your problem, it ain't here. I am getting mine, I am going to travel all the way from Hertford with it and I can get a tug just the same as you can, just put it in your motor".'

Terry had little sympathy for Kenny's paranoia about being pulled over by the police with gear in the boot, either. 'I will tell you what the soppy cunt wants, he wants a cab to pull up outside my daughter's house and bring it in.'

Nothing gets Terry more riled up than any threat of his innocent daughter being implicated in this stuff somehow.

'Yeah, he does,' Danny frowned.

'Yeah, go and bollocks,' spat Terry fiercely.

Danny was back onto practical matters, trying to dial down the tension a little bit. 'I can meet you up that hill Monday at 7 o'clock. That's perfect, innit? Up there 7 o'clock.'

On the same day, Terry and Danny had another very revealing little chat about Basil and his share of the loot.

Terry said about Basil, 'Think of what he has got at the moment, right he's got that gold, some of that gold.'

Danny agreed, 'Yeah.'

Terry followed up, 'I don't know what it comes to.' Danny quickly replied, 'Three hundred on the floor, Kenny said.'

Terry was doing mental calculations in his head. 'And he's got 70, weren't it?'

Danny corrected him: '80, 90 grand or something.'

Terry came straight back to him, having worked it out: '82 grand, just forget that he's got nothing else but that, how long's that going to last him?'

Danny was his usual assured self. 'For ever Tel, that will last him right through, he goes for the cheapest gaffs.'

Terry agreed. 'That foreign money he fucking won will probably last him ten years.'

When Terry made reference to Basil winning foreign money in a portion of the transcripts which was made public, many press sources mistakenly took it to mean that Basil had enjoyed the good fortune of a win on Euromillions or something similar abroad. The truth, as is often the case, was far simpler and came down to needing an understanding of the way that the criminals talked to each other. The 'foreign money he fucking won' was simply the foreign currency he had helped himself to during the divvy-up.

Danny was thinking fast. 'Do you know what, I don't want to be paranoid or nothing but you know all those 50-pound notes, they were all new, weren't they Tel?'

Terry concurred. 'Yeah they looked new, I found them.'

Danny: 'Brand new.'

'Did that come out of one box?' Terry questioned

Danny agreed with his usual, 'Yeah.'

Terry sounded unsure. 'But that was different packets I was taking it out of.'

Danny was taking the intellectual lead this time. 'No, they came out of one box. I'll tell you what he lost shall I? £1.6 million worth of gold he lost plus £70,000 in notes, he's lost a chunk that cunt there.'

Terry circled back to the key issue in hand – their loot. 'So what's that our way?'

Danny was warming to his theme, 'Well he's saying

350 for gold, say 33, say £1 million so he has lost £1 million worth of gold and £70,000 in cash, one box.'

These slightly odd figures exemplify the confusion over the value of the haul at this point, and showcase a typically 'Danny' combination of slightly delirious fantasising combined with the struggle of evaluating the box contents accurately.

Terry shook his head slightly in pity and disbelief. 'I feel a bit sorry, don't you?

Danny laughed, flashing his characteristic slightly dark sense of humour. 'Give it back to him!'

Terry laughed too. 'Give it back to him!!'

Danny had been watching the news very carefully, particularly the testimonies of the aggrieved depositors. He told Terry, 'They are all getting together now to sue the police. I'll tell you what, it's left a mystery that bit of work, there's 70 boxes and they'll think straight away [we've] gone in there for one thing only, I would.'

I wonder, not for the first or the last time, whether I am being played on this point. The inference that Basil was only after the contents of one box. It feels too neat, too filmic to be true. And the way that Danny talks about it off guard in the undercover recordings indicates that it is a wind-up.

'Yeah', Terry agreed.

Danny had started thinking in a new, mischievous direction, too. 'I'd say you got blackmail paperwork there on someone high profile or there was something like, fucking a mental bit of jewellery there…'

In any case, Danny could see the downside as well as the upside of discovering something of extraordinary worth or explosive importance, which would have created even more heat for them from the police and the vault box owners.

As he indicated to Terry, 'It would have been the biggest headache ever in your life, Tel.' Danny grinned and continued, 'Yeah, you would have to move away and take drugs or something, to get back to normality.'

'You would have,' Terry said solemnly.

Danny was fantasising about huge diamonds. 'If the prize was three bits of things as big as that, three of them, and you know, you got to re-cut em and you got £5 million a piece, it's easy done, ain't it?'

Terry was still agreeing with Danny and then the men's minds roved back to another job from their past.

'God knows what was in that other gaff, Tel,' Danny started quietly.

'Dan, it would have made this one look stupid,' mused Terry.

'One box would have probably been more than all them boxes in there,' Danny speculated, impressed all over again as he recollected.

'Unbelievable,' nodded Terry.

Danny couldn't quite get over the hoard they had witnessed at this other treasure trove. I have not been given a clear indication of where this treasure trove was though. 'It would have [frightened] the fucking life out of ya, I'll tell you that now, cos they are all riff-raff down there.'

Danny and Terry didn't like entanglements with dangerous gangsters. Who can blame them?

'Yeah, they are,' Terry clasped his hands nervously.

'Up there you're talking about serious...' continued Danny, glancing from side to side theatrically.

'You're talking about those cunts who get 200 grand out just to go to the casino.' Skint Terry certainly didn't include himself in this profligate criminal bracket.

'Yeah, that's it!' Danny liked the vivid snapshot that Terry had created.

A few days later Danny and Terry were stressing, specifically about Basil's gear.

Terry tried to stand firm. 'I'll say, well, that's Basil's problem, ain't it?'

'It's not our problem,' agreed Danny.

'I'm not looking after Basil's gear,' Terry frowned.

'He's got to take it,' agreed Danny. 'Take it back where... you know.'

'Yeah.' Terry knew.

Danny reiterated, 'We don't want it around us, that means he has got to come all the way over again and do a double journey, put it back where you had it.'

'We got two weeks there, then we want it all out,' Terry stated.

'Want it all out this week, Tel,' Danny clarified firmly.

Time and again, Danny has come back to the point of expressing his frustration that they didn't, for all that effort, get more boxes in the vault open. He is tantalised, intrigued and slightly tortured by the possible contents of the rest of the boxes. He always will be. He started thinking in 'If only' terms. *If only they had got in the first night; if only they had known the cases were bolted to the floor and the wretched pump had not broken*; and *if only they had extra pairs of hands, and the extra energy and enthusiasm*. It could have been amazing. It truly would have been the biggest robbery in modern history.

Danny and Terry were caught on camera on

Monday 18 May moving bins into Danny's driveway. Meanwhile, Kenny paid Hugh Doyle's workshop a visit, next to the Old Wheatsheaf in Enfield. Like several of the gang's other favoured haunts, it is a classic unassuming Victorian boozer with wooden benches outside and some slightly miserable-looking hanging baskets.

It seems as though Kenny thought of using Hugh's place to offload some of the loot. A meeting was then held to see if Terry and Danny were happy with that arrangement.

Let's allow Danny and Terry to speak for themselves on this important point, though.

Terry wanted to know, 'If he [Kenny] thought of his place yesterday why didn't he go over there yesterday, to have to drive over there Sunday, lovely day. He ain't got a fucking brain, has he?'

Danny concurred, 'He's starting to forget, the cunt.'

'He's done, ain't he?' Terry despaired.

Danny wasn't so sure. 'Only when he wants to forget,' he observed shrewdly.

Terry had focused back on the loot. 'Yeah, take it into his house. Get the cab driver to pull up.'

'Pretend like you're going on holiday,' agreed Danny, getting into the charade.

Terry had a good practical point. 'That cab's a van anyway, no problem just bring them out...'

Danny finished his mate's sentence for him '...and just walk round the corner with 'em.'

'We don't want a stick-up, now do we,' Terry cautioned wisely.

There was certainly quite a lot of anguish, even amongst these savvy and experienced thieves, about how to pass some of the loot on and monetise it.

So much anguish, in fact, that Danny and Terry had a tense back and forth on the subject. It was Terry who grasped the nettle and kicked off the difficult discussion.

'So the geezer goes, I've seen me. We're connected. You know. So I've got to be double fucking careful.' He lowered his voice even further. 'I can't go to who I normally go to.'

Danny, as he often does, tried to defuse the tension by being practical. 'Well, listen, he's gonna give us a price is he? On it, on it, is he? On them few. Well, we'll see what he comes back with... don't jump the gun now.'

The men were so twitchy about being overheard they were virtually murmuring under their breath.

Terry picked up the thread. 'Frank said, what I said to him, look tell me the truth. The price is what you're gonna get given. If it's accepted, it's a yay, if it ain't accepted, it's a no. So basically it's as simple as that. What would you say that parcel there is? Normal run of the day stuff, yeah?

Danny ran over the parcel contents aloud. 'Yeah, some nice little bits there. You know good high quality. You know what I mean, it's all sellable gear, it's all good gear.'

They were knee-deep in a discussion of the loot now. Danny was carrying on 'Yeah, yeah... them two fucking bags, the first two bags went under them stairs. So he took three bags into there. Gold.'

Terry was more focused on his vivid recollections of the physical discomfort of dragging the loot around. 'Look, think about what we had. I struggled up the stairs with one bag.'

Danny grinned at his old friend mischievously. 'You don't struggle with three bags, do you?'

Terry harked back to the nuts and bolts of the bag contents. 'No, it can't be just fucking all that gear we had in two bags can it? Nine carat [is] non-existent now – the only thing I picked up was nine carat.'

Danny was also questioning the quality. 'Not good indication you see.'

Terry continued for both of them. 'What I'm saying is, nine carat, he's fucking out of date, Dan. He's fucking out of date. If you've got a diamond worth 100 quid, right, if you've got a diamond worth 10,000 grand, what you gonna set it in? What's your shank gonna be?'

Danny had a swift response: '18 or platinum.'

Terry nodded quickly. '18 or platinum, if you've got a diamond worth 200 quid what you gonna put it in?'

'Nine carat,' replied Danny.

'Nine carat, innit?' Terry nodded again. You ain't gonna make the shank worth more than the stone.'

Danny was also nodding now. 'If you've got a fantastic beautiful stone you ain't gonna put it in a nine carat.'

'Course you ain't,' said Terry. 'But if you got a 200 pound stone you ain't gonna put it in an 18-carat shank that's worth more than the stone, are you? Even I know that and I'm a fucking dope.' Terry is anything but a dope, but this is typical of his self-deprecation.

After talking over some of the rings they had, thoughts turned to Brian.

As Terry said, 'The very first thing, I done with Brian. Oh, fucking trays of the cunts.'

'And who did he sell the parcel to?' Danny wanted to know.

Terry explained. 'He sold some and I sold some to

Frank. But the ones he sold, he said we'll get a price and I'll give you the money.'

The men were working through some murky details, not to mention some errors of judgement. Later in the same conversation, Terry remarked that Paul, one of the gang's associates had 'seen someone inside the jewellery shop. He'll take the whole lot on sale or return, put it in his shop. I said, "silly cunt".'

Danny was disapproving. 'That's no good, is it?'

Terry recounted his response. 'You what, I said sale or return? He sells two rings next week and I get 50 quid.'

'He's fucking mental,' Danny snorted.

'I said you've got to be,' quipped Terry, continuing. 'I said and then a month later he shuts the shop and fucks off.'

Danny was contemptuous. 'That's why they're dinlows [fools], innit, it's cos they don't want it round them Tel.'

The loot was clearly a very hot potato indeed. Terry's mind turned back to one of his co-conspirators again. 'So would Kenny. He don't know where that gear is tonight. Kenny don't know where that gear is. When he said Bill, I thought he said Bill's house.'

Danny agreed. 'I thought Bill's house, didn't you?'

So did I, yeah.' said Terry.

Danny pondered. 'Yeah, but he said Bill's gone away, can't get in.'

Terry was keeping up. 'But Bill give it to someone else.'

'Shouldn't have done that mate,' Danny said vehemently, remembering.

Terry was very direct. 'Kenny don't know where that gear is. Same as before, we're sitting in that restaurant and our gear is in the fucking Land Rover. He's a cunt.'

Danny was keen to make his feelings known. 'I shall tell him Monday, I'll say, Ken I'm not happy. I shall say that gear, you don't know where it is.'

'Bill knows where it is,' Terry recalled.

Danny was withering. 'Bill knows where it is. That's no fucking good. It ain't his gear, is it?'

'No, it's our gear,' snapped Terry. 'That's why we can't say to him. I was thinking, if you say to him it's *your* responsibility he's going to say well no it ain't. It's our gear. But you can't change it over in the road. If Bill brings it back to his house, slide it straight in his car and bring it over…'

Danny was on board with this solution. 'Well, we'll tell him that.'

HATTON GARDEN

Little did Danny, Terry and Kenny know, that far, far more of their activity with the loot was under scrutiny at this point.

CHAPTER TEN

THE SURVEILLANCE

'You've got to treat everyone as an enemy.'

(Danny)

Ｆrom very early on in the investigation, the police were having twice-daily meetings, morning and evening, to discuss their progress on the CCTV findings. They had several different CCTV systems at 88–90 Hatton Garden to trawl through – painstaking and tedious work. There was the communal CCTV, operated by the building owners. This basically covered the ground floor area with two cameras and, with another two cameras, the rear courtyard by the iron stairs to the Greville Street entrance. There was also a fifth camera which covered the first floor's flat roof.

The monitor and the hard drive for the communal CCTV were located in Carlos Cruse's office, two doors away from the Hatton Garden vault. Within the vault were five further cameras: two inside the vault, two outside it, and a fifth watching the front door to HGSD. The internal CCTV recorder was mounted in the cupboard within the airlock.

The police soon established, though, that the CCTV systems for the vault and building had been deactivated. However, there was a camera that was not shut down, located inside the corridor leading from the passageway to Greville Street. This camera was not part of the building CCTV. It was a separate, motion-sensitive system owned by Berganza Jewellers. The camera had its shortcomings as I have noted, but it still turned out to have its uses in capturing the robbers' comings and goings.

Another business on the second floor of the building had its own CCTV camera in the corridor, and this one captured Basil and Terry who briefly went to the second floor to deal with the lift. The police realised on viewing it that the robbers re-entered the building a second time. It was this camera that provided the incriminating footage of Danny emerging from the fire escape carrying the 'Clarke' pump and hose with a red handle and the 'Sealey' hydraulic pump that was left inside the vault. This led the police to speculate that something must have gone wrong on the first night, which had resulted in the need to leave and source another pump. By a canny process of deduction, this prompted the police to set up a search across London for recent purchases of Clarke pumps.

Both mornings, the robbers' van was captured arriving and leaving on a street camera. The police ran face and biometric analysis of the internal Berganza video. But there are some images of the gang from other CCTV systems mounted on surrounding buildings which show that they came back a second night.

Strikingly, the Berganza camera captured Brian sporting a very distinctive scarf and pair of stripy socks. In another bit of footage, Danny can be seen entering the building carrying a new box with a Sealey pump inside. The police extrapolated from that image that it was a fresh purchase.

Police identified that 25 Hatton Garden was used as look-out station, located opposite 88–90 on the other side of the crossroad between Greville Street and Hatton Garden. Like 88–90, it has two entrances: one from 25

Hatton Garden and one from 8–9 Greville Street. It overlooks both entrances to 88–90. The building has two proprietors, and is managed by Howell Brooks & Partners, one of the oldest London firms of Chartered Surveyors. It has 11 tenants. The owners have keys to the property, as do a number of contractors. Tenants have given keys to many of their employees.

Automatic number plate recognition (ANPR), as I have already briefly alluded to, was going to be a critical factor in catching our gang. Central London has a uniquely dense population of both number plate recognition cameras and CCTV, and a whole police department is dedicated just to ANPR.

ANPR is often all about identifying patterns. Were there any vehicles suddenly coming in and out of Hatton Garden in the preceding weeks and months, enough to cause suspicion? The police found footage of the gang's white van coming and going, and they discovered that it had false numberplates. They released the footage to the media.

The white van's route was traced to Cheshunt and Islington, but Danny and Terry were not overly worried watching the news – there was a shot of them getting in and out of the van, sure, but they had used false plates then disposed of the van. It wasn't traceable. Meanwhile, even though Terry in particular was worried about DNA traces and any forensic sloppiness at the centre, the police were still far off the scent when it came to the robbers' identities.

Even over a month later, in mid-May, Danny and Terry were still basking in the idea that the police were looking in all the wrong places. Danny indicated to Terry that what was 'going around the police, the old bill, was that it was an inside job.'

This news obviously came as a relief to Terry, who theorised about the police work, 'They will not put 100 per cent into it, cos they'll think, "You're mugging us off you cunts, you want us running all around London when it's fucking from inside."'

Danny agreed and described what his contact had told him the police were saying. 'He said all them are thinking, it's one of our own, that's what's going around. Do you know what's fucked them up and all?

'What?' said Terry.

Danny leaned back. 'Opening 70 boxes.'

Terry nodded slowly. 'I know.'

Danny tapped the side of his nose. 'That they cannot work it out.'

Terry leaned in closer. 'No they can't work that out… the biggest robbery that could have ever ever been.'

Danny agreed. 'That will never ever happen again.'

Terry continued. Danny was still with him. 'The biggest robbery in the fucking world we was on and that cunt...'

Terry hesitated as the topic of Brian Reader opened up but Danny encouraged him to go on: 'Yeah, Terry?'

Terry took a breath. 'The whole fucking 12 years I've been with him, three, four bits of work, fucked every one of them.'

Danny thumped his hand on the side of the table for emphasis. 'And he would have fucked this if we walked away with him.'

Terry nodded again. 'Course we would have.'

Danny said, 'If we didn't say, "Oh come on, we will have another go..."'

Terry was hanging on Danny's words. 'Yeah we would have been absolutely fucked, I would have, fucking hell.'

Danny had a very clear, and subsequently ironic, view of what fate would have been awaiting him. 'And I would have probably gone back to fucking low-life screwing and got nicked.'

Terry's vision of his alternative future was not any rosier. 'Well I would have been with you; any fucking thing would do me. At least what I've done, I've paid for my daughter's holiday. I've made sure they are alright, with their holidays and what not, not all that I wanted to give 'em, but let's see what we get once we chop it up, we will have half a clue. You can't plan on doing anything until you know what you got, can you?'

Danny's instinct, as always, was to support his old friend Terry. 'No, come on son, yeah, course you would, come on Tel.'

Terry was gruffly pleased with his reply, 'Come on', almost choking in his throat. Swerving away from the moment getting too bloody soppy, Danny had a bone to pick with another deserter.

'He must be cursing himself, that cunt.'

'Who?' asked Terry.

Danny folded his arms. 'That Carl.'

Terry gathered himself, readily acquiesced and gleefully elaborated. 'He must be thinking of committing suicide.'

Danny pondered. 'I'm trying to put myself in his mind, forget about everything, I'm him. The bloke would be sitting at the airport. I bet he is boozing now, smoking that shit now. Unless he has seen the light.'

The patient, methodical surveillance captured some very significant material on Friday, 10 April, because this was the first evidence of the gang getting together again, either over the phone or in person, since the heist ended five days before. Danny rang Kenny from an area in the north of Islington. Then Kenny's Mercedes was spotted and logged on City Road at 12.49pm and on Rosebery Avenue/Mount Pleasant at 12.54pm using ANPR.

There was a flurry of phone calls between Terry, Kenny and Danny. This is the day that Brian came back in via Kenny. It seems reasonably likely that Kenny was with Brian at Scotti's Snack Bar, where they appear to meet every Friday, and Danny was with Terry in The Castle pub down the road.

To a certain extent, these calls were just about the gang pooling their knowledge of what the police knew already, but a lot of the calls took place in Clerkenwell, near to Hatton Garden, so there was something else going on as well. They were trying to figure out how to sell on the loot. Were they cutting some kind of deal?

As I've already said, the gang had a guy called Frank, although he turned out to be somewhat difficult to manage as a buyer. All of them were blinded by Frank's science. It was all very stressful and confusing for Danny and Terry.

THE SURVEILLANCE

In a conversation about Frank, which was completely typical in tone, Terry freely expressed his insecurity about taking items to Frank that he had valued incorrectly.

As Terry said, 'What I am saying is, I may be right, but if you take it to someone like Frank, he would laugh at me.'

'Yeah, he would,' Danny acquiesced solemnly.

Terry continued, imitating Frank's impatient tones. 'He'd say, "Oh fucking shut up, fucking hell. What do you want for it – six grand? You fucking mental." You know what I mean?'

Danny strove to be pragmatic. 'It's worth what it is in gold.'

'Yeah.' Terry tugged at his shirt sleeve, nodding.

'There were diamonds there...' Danny continued.

Terry tried to imagine it in some kind of comprehensible context. 'It's got to be made for a dress thing, ain't it Dan, like a dress?'

Danny saw wisdom in Terry's argument. 'The more I think of it, it's antique, Tel.'

'Yeah,' Terry concurred.

'You know what I mean,' said Danny. 'It's 70, 80 years old.'

The more disappointing aspects of the haul, as well

as their long history, had made the two men cynical. Terry knew some of the gear wasn't worth what they had hoped though, especially in Frank's eyes. In Frank's defence, he had been shafted in the past and landed with gear he couldn't shift. Once bitten, twice shy, perhaps.

Danny tried to insert a more hopeful note. 'See how you get on with Frank.' Terry nodded.

Danny carried on. 'And to say, look, I'll send the parcel.'

Terry rubbed his hands together. 'Once it's all sorted I know what I'm going to sell first.'

'Yes.' Danny was equally fired up.

Terry outlined his plan. 'And I can take it over to Frank and I'll say, what will you give me for that, mate? He might say, "Give me a couple of weeks and I'll sort it all out".'

Danny agreed vociferously.

'Then he will tell me,' Terry went on, 'and I say to you, he's given me that.'

'Yeah.' Danny drained his cup of tea and leaned in.

'And obviously our parcels would be similar, won't they,' Terry said knowingly.

Danny agreed again.

'Or what we stick in the middle that we can't sell…,' Terry mused.

'Well, that's got to go to him anyway,' Danny said firmly.

Terry had the last, optimistic, note of hope on the matter. 'I'll say, "What you reckon about that?" Whatever he says about that, let's hope it's about a million pounds!'

Terry could certainly use the money. At this point in time they must have felt very confident they'd got away with it. The police only had a few grainy shots and no forensics.

On Saturday, 11 April, however, the game changed for both the police and villains. Up until then, the gang had been unaware for sure that the police net was closing in on them, but Danny and Terry were certainly keeping a very close eye out for even the slightest mention of the case in the media. Danny was scouring the news outlets every day. I would assume that Basil was doing the same from whatever foreign location he was sunning himself in with his ill-gotten gains. Danny and Terry were tempted to do the same. Although they were spending an awful lot of time convincing themselves, and each other, that it was going to be impossible for the police to work out who they were, doubt and uncertainty were creeping in. Plus they were having a nightmare trying to sell the loot.

That fateful day, the *Daily Mirror* ran the headline 'The Diamond Geezers' and published CCTV images of six masked men, who they dubbed: Mr Ginger, Mr Strong, Mr Montana, The Gent, The Tall Man and The Old Man. Basil did not feature. Another image from a CCTV camera in the street showed a white Ford Transit van pulling up to the alley beside the building. Again they hinted that the thieves must have had inside help as there was no sign of forced entry to the building. This revelation effectively blew the police's concealed line of enquiry, and resulted in a blanket refusal to feed the media information.

Details gleaned from the video were also run by the Flying Squad's bank of underground informants and other sources within the criminal fraternity. They hoped that the striking pair of smart shoes and striped socks worn by 'The Gent' might give them a name. Another key item was the hoodie bearing the word Montana by another gang member. Shit.

The gang were absolutely horrified. Suddenly their conviction that they had been cautious enough to evade detection seemed fatally naïve. In this new nightmare scenario it was very much a matter of when, not if, they got recognised by someone.

Danny and Terry were frustrated with Brian and

Basil at this turn of events too. The methodical, almost OCD, attention to detail was their domain. Danny and Terry were bigger-picture gang members and dealing with 'other shit'. What were Brian and Basil playing at letting this incriminating footage come into existence?

There was another painful issue running in tandem and also generated by the media coverage. The *Daily Mirror* had labelled the police 'Keystone Cops' for what was perceived to be a bungling failure to answer the alarm and so far getting nowhere with the investigation. While this did not reflect the significant breakthroughs that the police had made behind the scenes, it had got their backs up, and it did Danny and Terry no favours.

When I asked retired superstar police officer Tom Manson about this, he had strong views. Tom made a series of revelations about how damaging some less ethical representatives of the media were in the aftermath of the job. He told me that they followed the police around Hatton Garden and tried to buy CCTV evidence from local shops and businesses. He also talked about the 'Keystone Cops' headline.

That was absolutely a low moment in the investigation and a political and public relations nightmare. But the police had remained focused. They had shut out all the noise and speculation. Instead, they spent days and nights painstakingly searching through ANPR camera footage and CCTV looking for any clues, running every number plate and delving into everything that might be conceivably suspicious.

That process reaped very significant dividends just under a week after the robbery.

The team sifting through the CCTV surveillance footage spotted another vehicle driven slowly through Hatton Garden on the second night of the raid. It was a Mercedes with a black roof and alloy wheels. CCTV footage of two men exiting that Mercedes matched camera images of Danny and Carl, captured on Thursday not just on Greville Street, but at the fire escape door.

When the investigating team ran the registration numbers through their ANPR system, the Mercedes had been picked up driving through Hatton Garden on numerous occasions in the months before the raid. It always ended up in north London, following a similar route to the white van. Another red flag, and odd detail, was that the Mercedes appeared to be falsely registered to an individual in Wales.

From Monday, 13 April onwards a really frantic effort was underway to find the Mercedes in north London.

THE SURVEILLANCE

It was all hands on deck and the police were working through the night. A deep dive into call data and cell site analysis to get a picture of Kenny's connections and movements went on for days. The police applied to the court to get a judge to sanction planting a bug in the Mercedes.

Then came another breakthrough. Surprise, surprise, it was the impetuous and unplanned purchase of the pump. Police inquiries confirmed the sale of the pump thanks to two pieces of evidence. The first was an invoice in Machine Mart for the purchase of the pump. There it was for all to see – Danny's signature of V. Jones and his street address. The second was CCTV of Danny in DM Tools, a Twickenham hardware store near Machine Mart.

Not for the first or last time, Danny's distinctive clothing landed him in it, too. He was wearing a similar hoodie to the one he was seen wearing in footage of the raid. And extremely bright blue shoes. The Mercedes parked outside didn't go unnoticed either.

Hugh and Kenny met at the Moon Under Water in Enfield, unaware they were being watched, trying to work out what to do with the stuff. The police were struggling to get anywhere with Kenny. He seemed like a bit of an empty vessel to them, no mates, no regular drinking buddies, no one he played golf or cards or watched football with.

On Friday, 17 April, Brian Reader was spotted exiting Farringdon station, again using the Freedom Card under his pseudonym. Surveillance tracked Kenny to Scotti's Snack Bar where he met Brian Reader. Sat outside, a suspicious individual soon joined them, carrying a Waitrose carrier bag and wearing a brown suit. He showed them what was inside the carrier bag. Police didn't know who the guy in the brown suit was, and at this stage they hadn't identified Brian either.

Interestingly, there was no sign of any mobile usage for this meeting. It just seemed to be a regular Friday thing, totally innocuous to the untrained eye; just some old guys have a drink and chatting.

To me, the mobile phone usage in the run-up, during and in the aftermath of the heist seems of potentially huge significance. Police sources I have spoken to corroborate this to the extent that they will not tell me if Basil had a mobile phone, as one replied, 'No knowledge and still all part of the police investigation so can't comment.' Fortunately a gang member had already let slip that Basil did have a mobile phone with him.

I also asked one police source if the gang had separate

mobile phones that they spoke on about the job? Or did they use their regular, own mobiles throughout and after? He shook off the question, telling me that it wasn't something he could discuss, although one of the grainier surveillance photos in the public domain could be of one gang member looking at what appears to be an old-fashioned Nokia-type phone. This could indicate that they owned separate mobile phones that they used to talk about the job.

In the meantime, Billy came back from his holiday.

Brian Reader was steadily, doggedly trying to work his way back in. His simplest route was through the weaker links in the chain like Kenny. Divide and rule, as I was discovering from nearly everybody, is very much Brian Reader's modus operandi. Danny and Terry were significantly less receptive.

In Danny's view, after Brian had walked off the job, Brian was a 'fucking wanker, regardless of his age.'

Terry agreed. 'Fucking wanker.'

'He looked defeated just when he sat in that chair,' recalled Danny, thinking back to Brian's demeanour on a resting break during the first night.

'Yeah he did,' agreed Terry.

Danny continued, 'Years ago he started that up again. I said to him the other day, you're 40 years behind, Brian. You can see what a selfish man he's been though, can't you?'

This theme of Brian being defeated had come up frequently in my meetings with Jon and Val. His frailty, his multiple health complaints and his personal struggle with adjusting to his unwelcome status as a widower, rattling around his luxurious house in Kent by himself, popping pills.

As night follows day, it was time for a *Crimewatch* appeal on the evening of 23 April 2015. A surprisingly stingy £20,000 reward was offered for information leading to the arrest and conviction of the gang responsible. Scotland Yard also made an appeal to the wives and girlfriends of anyone who know how to use a heavy-duty drill. Detective Superintendent Craig Turner, head of the Flying Squad, said: 'We are keen to hear from wives or partners of anyone who has specialist knowledge or skills that use this sort of equipment. Were they away during the Easter bank holiday weekend or have they been acting oddly since the burglary was carried out?'

While certain elements of the press were mocking the police for their handling of the case, and even ridiculing them for the low amount of reward money on offer for such a major crime, law enforcement were actually being extremely wily at this point, not to mention showing the willingness to play a long game. There was also a cleverly disingenuous element to Craig Turner's statement, because thanks to the surveillance, the police knew a lot more at this point than they were willing to let on. This way, the police tell me, the criminals were more likely to get sloppy and slip up.

Back in the surveillance video and audio came evidence of the hapless Kenny in the City Road area on Friday, 24 April calling Terry. This call was identified by the police accessing the Mecca Bingo Islington cell site. ANPR spotted his Mercedes on City Road at the same time.

We know that Kenny met up with Danny and Terry at the Ye Olde Cherry Tree Pub in Southgate. Ye Olde Cherry Tree is a centuries-old coaching inn that has been through many different incarnations before its most recent one as a gastropub. The Travelodge next door to it adds to its strong sense of anonymity, a meeting place where you can rapidly disappear among a bustling, diverse north London crowd. Despite some nods to the 21st century, it retains the rather quaint interior and old-world beer garden which the gang members seem to find particularly beguiling.

Kenny, Danny and Terry then moved on to the Highland Angus Steakhouse in Cannon Hill, Southgate. Founded in 1971, the steakhouse was a luxury when the gang members were young, but these days it was the epitome of naff. Nevertheless, this place harboured a nostalgic feeling for them.

Crimewatch was the leading conversation topic. The paltry nature of the reward had them all amused and affronted in equal measure. In retrospect, the gang can't believe at this meal that they were metaphorically slapping each other on the backs for evading capture and congratulating themselves on just how little the police seemed to know or understand about the perpetrators. Of course, the reality was that by this point, their every move was being watched.

After the meal, the three men went together to have a look in the boot of Terry's Citroën Saxo. It's likely that what they were looking at is the gold smelter we know he was driving about with. They once again talked through the contents of the holdalls and how to put them back together again.

Meanwhile the police had positively connected Brian Reader with the Brink's-Mat robbery at Heathrow in 1983. This was the point when they realised they were chasing a potential accessory to murder, because of

Detective Fordham's brutal death during Brink's-Mat, as well as a vault robbery. This created an emotional and moral angle for many of the police involved that had been absent before. This gang could be a nasty lot. They also made a firm connection with Terry's involvement in the Security Express depot robbery, also in 1983.

The police were by no means ready to show their hand yet, and were wholly unwilling to bow to the media's demand for quick wins and broadcasting of every lead or minor result. Instead they applied to bug Terry's Citroën Saxo.

The digital police detective work was ongoing and intensive. They were already recording in Kenny's car. Even so, some of what the criminals were doing at this point remains very mysterious.

We do know that on Tuesday, 28 April, Kenny collected Danny and Terry in the morning from Danny's home. Danny was wearing the same gear that he wore when he bought the pump and hose in Twickenham.

The Mercedes arrived in an unnamed road running parallel with the River Lea; they got out of the car and walked along the canal. They visited the Narrow Boat Café at the Marina in Lea Valley, near Enfield, where they stayed until noon. From the café, which is out of the way, you can see anyone approaching. There's only one way in over a canal bridge. This is a very definite anti-surveillance move. Or at the very least they didn't want to be overheard. The gang have told me that they were really worried by now.

On the evening of 1 May, Kenny drove Terry to The Castle pub in Clerkenwell, next to Farringdon Station and a very short walk away from Hatton Garden. This was the highly significant first face-to-face meeting between Brian and Terry since the robbery had taken place, and they spent the evening together. Brian came into this meeting truly gunning to get involved again.

The police have indicated that a spy camera was placed to record them. The police also employed a specialist undercover lip-reader to aid them in deciphering what was being said. The police, after some of the bad PR earlier in the investigation, were very keen to marshal as much concrete evidence as possible before they moved in to make an arrest.

As we know Brian Reader wasn't there on the second night of the robbery, so there is no reason for him to have known in detail what had taken place. Terry described the moment they breached the vault with great satisfaction to Brian, and walked him through the operation of the pump and hose and even the noise of the cabinets falling over. Terry was grandstanding in front of Brian, filling him in on all the juicy stuff he missed after he decided to abandon the job, and he was going to savour every second.

Brian had precious little time for Terry's big talk and wanted to get down to the nitty gritty. It was his plan, his job, and he wanted to be properly compensated for his trouble. Terry pushed back hard. It was Brian who had walked off the job. All the bad blood and jostling for position between these two angry old men came to the fore in this meeting.

Terry, Danny and Kenny were all in touch with one another throughout the day. This was clear from the subsequent intensive police surveillance of Kenny's car, including his incriminating mobile phone conversations inside the car. Indeed, Kenny's white Mercedes E200 had provided the very first big break in the surveillance, after the police CCTV team noticed Kenny's car driving through Hatton Garden a dodgy number of times over the weekend of the robbery. ANPR had allowed the police to trace the car not just to Kenny's house but to identify it on Kenny and

Danny's pump-shopping trip in Twickenham, too. This was particularly important as it confirmed the pump purchaser as Danny Jones (with a long history of armed robbery, burglaries, break-ins and possession) and connected him to the robbery.

The police used a comprehensive analysis of the mobile data to work out that the Carl being mentioned was Carl Wood. But Basil was a much tougher nut to crack, at least according to the official police line that there was no record of any phone calls between Basil and the gang members. However, I know that Basil did have a mobile with him on the job, so I suspect this is a whitewash. In any case, all the police were willing to admit at this point was that they had worked out that Basil was the expert on alarms.

In the early afternoon of Friday, 8 May, Kenny, Terry and Danny met as usual and sat outside Scotti's Snack Bar. Unusually, just the three of them met there with no Brian in tow.

Kenny later drove to Hatton Garden with Brian Reader as a passenger, having probably collected him from Farringdon station. Back at the scene of the crime, they met up with a man whom PC Steel, an observing officer, described as having 'Elvis-style large gold-rimmed glasses'. Could this have been

Basil? Perhaps in another silly disguise rather like his ginger wig?

Kenny, Terry and Danny met up again down the pub in the late afternoon. Then they moved on to Bonnie Gull Seafood Shack in Exmouth Market. The Bonnie Gull is now closed, which is rather a shame, because it served British seaside nostalgia fare and had 20 attractive outside dining tables. It was a pleasant place to tuck into fish and chips and watch the world go by, and for the gang it was one of the few places that seemed to offer a genuine Clerkenwell rival to their beloved Scotti's.

Terry's Saxo was later spotted returning on the A10. Footage also revealed that Kenny met up with Brian Reader and an unidentified male outside Scotti's in Clerkenwell Green. Terry and Danny were seen travelling westbound.

The police had now successfully bugged Terry's car too, and were recording pretty devastating conversations in it.

Unfortunately for Danny, this meant that the police clearly heard him saying to Terry, 'The biggest cash robbery in history at the time and now the biggest Tom in the fucking world, that's what they are saying … and what a book you could write, fucking hell.'

Tom is Cockney rhyming slang for jewellery and was one way for the gang to talk about the raid discreetly, even when they were sat inside a private vehicle as they were now.

Later, Kenny met with Terry and Danny, driving them to The Castle in his Mercedes. There they met Brian Reader, and the four of them ate in the Delhi Grill restaurant in Chapel Market that evening.

Distinguished by its jaunty blue façade, the Delhi Grill is an unassuming little Indian canteen-style restaurant, known as a 'dhaba' in Punjabi. It serves an unpretentious but delicious take on street food. At first sight, its small, cramped table settings seem like an odd choice of venue for secretive conversations. But the gang valued it for its loud bustle and chatter, which drown out any conversations best not overheard.

Everyone took their own cut from the loot. However, each cut was not equal. This understandably caused controversy and intense discussion. Terry and Danny had become increasingly nervous and really disliked that the circle of trust had widened with the inclusion of Billy and Jon. At the Delhi Grill, they decided to amass everything again in one place: at Terry's daughter Terri's house on Sterling Road.

Kenny, Brian, Danny, and Terry left the Delhi Grill

and drove off in the Mercedes. Brian was dropped at Angel tube station. The police were really onto them now, with just days to go before the arrest.

ANPR picked up Terry taking his daughter Terri to the airport, for a holiday which he paid for. At Danny's house he and Danny are seen placing something in his boot. Terry then drove to Terri's house.

On arrival, Danny pulled a big plastic bucket out of the boot and carried it into Sterling Road. This unassuming container would later turn out to be stuffed with precious gems. He had no idea that he was being watched.

Terry's blue Citroën Saxo was sighted at the junction between Napier Road and Cropley Street in Islington. This junction provides the vehicle access to 14 Bletsoe Walk. At this point, Terry and Danny were in the vehicle. At the same time, Terry attempted to call Kenny but the call was forwarded; the cell site the phone utilised reveals his whereabouts being in the vicinity of Bletsoe Walk. Terry made two further brief calls to Kenny. Kenny then met with Danny and Terry at Bletsoe Walk. Kenny attempted to call Hugh but the call was forwarded to his voicemail. Hugh then called Kenny. The purpose of that call was to arrange Kenny's visit to Hugh's workshop later that same day.

In the surveillance Danny and Terry were clearly anxious about yet another person invading the circle of trust, in this instance, Hugh Doyle.

Terry warned Danny, tellingly after a discussion about prisons, 'Another one that knows, Hughie, he's a cunt ain't he? We've got a cab driver who knows [i.e. Jon], Hughie will know now. Don't fucking leave them bags with Hughie.'

Danny shook his head. 'He knows he's a complete cunt.'

'He does,' Terry agreed vociferously. 'They all know he is. Bill knows he is.'

'Yeah,' Danny agreed, then mumbled something to himself.

'Oh, Bill knows he is,' assured Terry. 'I don't know that Bill, but even looking at him and talking to him, I bet he knows he [Hugh] is fucking having him over.'

'Yes, we don't want Hughie to see us really,' said Terry.

'No,' agreed Danny.

'Cos he's going to tumble, Hughie,' Terry mused. 'He might think he's bought the gear.'

'Yeah,' agreed Danny.

'Depending on what he [Bill] tells him,' clarified Terry.

Danny muttered something again.

'And if he has left that longer than ten minutes Hughie will have something out of it,' continued Terry grimly.

'Yeah, you've got to treat everyone as an enemy,' Danny observed with an unusually high level of cynicism.

'You fucking have, Dan,' Terry agreed.

Meanwhile, on the surveillance, Kenny was sighted driving his Mercedes from Islington to Enfield to meet Hugh at his workshop. Danny and Terry drove to Enfield, too, in Terry's Saxo. Kenny called Hugh for 14 seconds; the cell site Kenny's phone utilised revealed his location as the neighbourhood of, but not at, 3 Windmill Hill.

On arrival, when Kenny opened his car door, Hugh said, 'Give me two minutes, I'll try to get rid of Dave [his employee]. I'll tell him to get a coffee or something.'

During this meeting with Hugh, Kenny called Terry for half a minute or so. The ever-hapless Kenny had a problem. 'I've got lost, I'm in Parsonage Lane. You know where that is? OK, alright mate, alright.' Kenny's dog was whining restlessly in the background as he drove on.

Terry was sitting with Danny in the Painter's Café at 131 The Chase, Parsonage Lane, Enfield. After leaving the café, Terry and Danny got into the Saxo and drove away.

Police recorded the following conversation within the Saxo, between Danny and Terry.

Danny said, 'Bill's bringing it over.'

Terry replied, 'What a fucking performance, now he's [Kenny's] got the cab driver [Jon] to pay, Bill, and now Hughie.'

Danny was brisk. 'That's his problem, ain't it?'

Terry was exasperated. 'But what I am saying is, oh fucking hell he can't... he can't keep a secret Dan can he?'

'No,' Danny replied.

Terry was thinking. 'So if I'd been in with Hughie, I would have said I brought it.'

'Brought some straight away,' Danny agreed.

Terry nodded. 'Hughie knows he's a buyer, I'd have said I brought some of the gear, end of innit. Kenny likes the idea that he was part of it.'

Danny sat up straighter. 'But I told ya, didn't I, but, that's alright if he kept it to himself and made something out of it.'

Terry agreed. 'Yeah.'

Kenny called Billy to update him as to the location and timing of the exchange. Billy called Jon then called Kenny back. Billy texted Jon the address of The Wheatsheaf. Although Jon deleted the memory on his phone, destroying the message, it was somehow recovered by the police from Billy's handset.

A sat nav from Jon's car also contained the location of The Wheatsheaf. In a run of bad luck for Jon, this was found when the sat nav was examined despite the fact that Jon had deleted the history on this device several times.

Conscious of possibly being under surveillance, Danny described a device to Terry that he had been shown by one of his relatives. Danny believed it could be used to counter any surveillance effort, and said his contact had told him, '"I got a good tool for you if you want it". I said, "What is it?" He said, "Fit it in your car, you can hide it, hide the aerial, it's a little black box like that and it will go bip bip bip bip bip... Old Bill 20 feet away from you, plain clothes, anything." He said it does, it goes up to half a mile, Old Bill in the vicinity.'

'Fuck me.' Terry shook his head in admiration at this marvellous-sounding piece of tech.

Danny wanted to keep explaining about it. 'So if

they come on you within half a mile that goes bip bip bip bip. As soon as they get closer it gets louder and louder. It's a good tool, ain't it? Nine hundred quid to have it fitted in your motor.'

It sounds like this would have been money very well spent for our gang of thieves...

Terry still couldn't quite believe it. 'What, that little black box tells you straight away?'

'If it's going all day, you know it's on ya,' Danny assured him.

'Yeah, fucking right,' Terry nodded.

'It does Tetra, Tetra radio, that's what the Old Bill are on, Tetra.'

Unfortunately for Danny and Terry, the police were on to them in many more ways than one, and they were closing in fast.

CHAPTER ELEVEN
THE ARREST

*'And there's the police again they keep pulling people…
The fucking Old Bill.'* (Terry)

The day of the arrest was Tuesday, 19 May 2015, not that the gang had the least inkling of that fact as the day started. Appropriately enough, in the middle of what was the coldest May for nearly 20 years, the day brought rain and thunderstorms.

At this point, though, perhaps the word 'gang' is inaccurate. The group of men had atomised, not just from the first night but also from the subsequent jostling over the divvy-up and the storing and selling on of some of the loot.

If there was one thing Danny and Terry didn't like, it was the sense of somebody pulling a fast one. Especially Terry, as he said of Brian's behaviour on the job, 'I know, what a cunt, when you think, what a cunt.'

Danny had his theory. 'I know that it's the badness in him, that's the unprofessionalism.'

Danny was weary of even these limited, antagonistic interactions, though. 'I don't want to see Brian no more, Tel,' he said.

Terry felt that there was unfinished business, however. This isn't surprising. I know from the gang and their associates that Terry had a much deeper relationship with Brian than Danny ever did. 'I do want to see him. I want to see him once, to say, "Brian, I told you that I want to wait to see what I've got, and what I've got is very, very disappointing down to you, so mate, you ain't on."'

There was so much bitterness lingering from the divvy-up, such a sense of injustice on Terry's part, always desperate for cash, that he had been deprived of his fair share.

Danny couldn't see any good reason why the others should be exonerated. He was happy to focus the lens on Brian but wanted the others to feel the heat, too. 'And tell the other geezers.'

Terry was in full agreement with Danny on this round of the endless blame game. 'The other geezers, if I ever see them, I'll say, "So it's down to you that I ain't got a nice few quid, you and Brian." What do you want me to say?'

'That other cunt, he's bad, isn't he?' Danny ventured.

Terry nodded rapidly. 'Yes he is.'

'The make-up man,' Danny said, leaning back.

'Who?' Danny had lost Terry a bit.

'Carl, the make-up man,' Danny expanded.

Terry was utterly dismissive. 'Oh, Carl, I think, Dan, I know there's nothing graceful in what Brian's done. Three and a half year's work and I ain't going back. There's nothing inspirational about that, they are both as bad as another as far as I am fucking concerned.'

'Yeah, you're right.' Danny was enjoying this now.

'Both as bad as one another,' Kenny stated.

'Both arseholes went,' Danny reiterated. 'In our world you either stay or you go.'

'You stay or you go, fucking end of story,' Terry emphasised. This was the basic code of honour these old school rogues lived by. Not all rules were made to be broken. Fate was, however, about to catch up with these men for some rules that had been broken.

The day of the arrest, first thing, Kenny Collins

picked up Danny for a trip to see Hugh on Windmill Hill in Enfield. As the two men got closer to Hugh's rear yard, Kenny Collins remarked, 'There's the Old Wheatsheaf, you might think the car park is round there but it ain't, it's round here.'

'Is Bill coming with it?' Danny wanted to know.

Kenny Collins replied, 'Yeah he's the one who's going to bring it out.' He mumbled something to himself. 'This is the car park, look, I'll park over there see. Oh he's... they're in.'

Billy, in blue jeans and a bright red hooded coat, pulled up and parked his black Audi soon afterwards before walking off towards Windmill Hill. He came back with a newspaper and sat in the car. So far, nothing out of the ordinary.

Danny and Kenny arrived in the Mercedes and talked to Billy. Danny was casually but nattily dressed as usual, a bit sporty, in beige shorts and a grey jumper. Kenny, more formal, wore a black jacket and dark trousers.

Danny, Kenny and Billy soon approached the exit to the car park while Hugh returned to his workshop. Just after 9.30am, Hugh, along with his employee Dave, came out of the premises and walked towards Hugh's Associated Response vehicle. Dave got in the vehicle and drove away. Hugh then got into his car and drove off with his wife. Danny and Kenny took the Audi.

The atmosphere was incredibly tense. They had a jittery taxi driver oblivious to what was being exchanged. Kenny was under massive pressure from Brian who was ringing and wanted to know what was going on with the gear.

Kenny drove his Mercedes into the car park. Helpfully for the subsequent investigation, he parked it with the boot partially in view of the CCTV camera. Shortly after, a red VW Golf drove into the car park. A white male dressed in a grey suit got out of the car, walked past the Mercedes and out of the car park. Who was this mystery man?

Jon's Mercedes taxi arrived. Billy approached the driver's window and talked to Jon, who wore a dark jacket with a white stripe down the arm. Jon got out and Danny and Kenny joined them by the vehicle. At this point Danny took out a black holdall and put it in the boot of the Mercedes. Billy took out a second holdall and handed it to Danny, who placed that in the Mercedes too, before Billy took another smaller holdall out of the taxi and shoved it into the boot. After a quick exchange with Jon who was moving towards the exit, Billy left the car park on foot and returned to his Audi.

Kenny drove off in the Mercedes with Danny in the front passenger seat. Danny and Kenny arrived at Terry's daughter Terri's house on Sterling Road in the Mercedes, carried the holdalls into the house and shut the door. All was still and quiet. Then, well, everything caught up with them.

At 9.55am, the police received their go sign. The front and the back of the house were covered.

Six police cars screeched to a halt outside the house. Officers in baseball caps and flak jackets leapt out of the vehicle and battered the front door in. The gang inside could hear them shouting 'Police! Get down!' at the top of their lungs.

Athletic Danny was first on his feet. 'FUCK.'

He couldn't resist the urge to leg it. Maybe all the hours spent in the gym were going to come to a sudden, very practical purpose. Two officers waiting for him out in the back garden weren't silly though. Danny barely made it out of the back patio doors. Adrenalin pumping through all three of them, Danny was shoved back inside.

Taken completely by surprise, Terry and Kenny froze. They were far less nimble on their feet than

Danny anyway. All the planning, danger, politicking and thieving had come to this. Two tired old men face down on the floor being cuffed.

Elsewhere that fateful morning, soon after 10am, police arrested Brian, Billy, Carl and Jon.

Billy Lincoln got pulled over by the police on the A10 in his black Audi. Billy described 'pandemonium' during his arrest to the jury during his trial, and said he was yelling, 'Argh, me fucking hips!' because the rough arrest was murder on his double hip replacement.

Val told me just how different the police's approach was to the 'old days'. She said, 'They used to smash the place up, tear everything apart. People would hide things where they could and there was a good chance the police wouldn't find them.'

Police work had moved on beyond belief. Now when they carried out a raid like this they were tooled up with the highest-quality gadgets available.

I also asked retired Chief Superintendent Tom Manson all about the searching of the houses once they were onto the gang. He described complex imaging equipment, dogs able to detect both drugs and cash, and how the police could make a small entry in a cavity wall and insert a small camera to search the space. The cops even had a drone above the house, scanners for the walls to detect anything hidden, a special machine that can detect whether any ground has been moved. All a long way from smashing down doors and ransacking the place, tactics now consigned to the past. The more Tom talked, the more it all felt like an old-fashioned crew being outgunned, outwitted and overwhelmed by the sheer technical knowhow and intelligence of today's police. I almost felt sorry for Danny, Terry and the others. Crime was clearly much harder than it used to be. As a villain in the outer circle of this gang said to me, 'It's all over, pal.'

Inside the holdalls and elsewhere at Sterling Road, a vast quantity of jewels were recovered. Precious stones including many sapphires and diamonds; top notch Breitling, Omega, Tag Heuer and Rolex wristwatches; rings (in both white and gold metal) and earrings, necklaces, bangles and brooches; two loupes (small magnifiers used to scrutinise jewellery), a set of electronic scales and numerous small white cardboard folders on the dining room table containing precious stones; a brown leather holdall full of tools and a graphite crucible for smelting gold.

Significantly, another container recovered was a pot of a number of Asian gold necklaces, bangles and pendants. Terry had made explicit reference to Indian gold when he explained on 15 May how he intended to dispose of it. 'I'm going to melt my good gold down … The Indian, the 18, that could be my pension if I could get half an idea of what's there, you know what I mean…'

The police also raided Danny and Val's house. During their search, they checked through all of Val's dresses. Val explained this to me, describing a very clever process called 'converting'. As she said, 'People will get real diamonds sown onto dresses to look like cheap diamante. Hiding in plain sight, so to speak.'

I loved the idea of this. I joked with her, wondering if there were any charity shop frocks up and down the country with priceless real diamonds sewn into them looking like tacky party dresses.

Val carried on, 'My favourite crystal lamp was taken down and apart by the police and each crystal was tested. I was telling them to stop, not because there was anything dodgy, but because I didn't want my favourite lamp spoiled! If there was treasure hidden in my house, those police were determined they were going to find it.'

The gang had not been that silly, though.

The police announced that they had found the book

DNA for Dummies when they raided Danny's house. However, that book was Val's not Danny's. The police were trying to make Danny look stupid whereas, in fact, she had bought it to learn about DNA after a close family member had died.

From reading the transcripts, though, I knew there was a lot more stashed throughout the house than was contained in the three holdalls. Where was it all? I was imagining woods and graveyards all around Enfield and Hertfordshire, innocent dog walkers, kids exploring and making dens, and in years to come, one of them stumbling across a bag of buried treasure. It was a childhood fantasy of mine and in this case it was probably true. Not that they would ever tell me where they had stashed it.

A few weeks after the robbery, though, Danny talked Terry through the whereabouts of some of the gear. As Danny said, 'On my life, Tel, remember I only took half a bag with me Tel, from that flat easy bag.'

There was a question it seemed Terry wanted answered as much as I did. 'The stones, where did you put them, with them or over the cemetery?'

Danny swiftly reassured him, basking in his skills. 'No, leave them up the cemetery… it's only a packet like that, ain't it? We will say that's our bit.'

'Yeah, like a carat,' said Terry eagerly.

Danny leaned over. 'You know what, Gospel truth here...' he lowered his voice and whispered in Terry's ear.

'We will have them,' said Terry.

Danny had a plan. 'I'll tell you what to do, cos there will be so many little articles each, I want to see how you'd get on with Frank.' Frank, the buyer, has something of a starring role in this drama.

'Frank,' Terry repeated.

Danny was cajoling a bit. 'Let him talk on your level first, right, then I'll say right I might as well fuck off now, you got to look after him, you know what I mean, the conversation... I'll say could you keep the gold for a week.'

Terry nodded sagely. 'Yeah I'd suppose he would do that.'

'Yeah,' Danny grunted.

'I'm going to melt my good gold down,' Terry stated decisively.

'What, your coins, the other stuff?', Danny wanted to know.

Terry nodded again. 'The Indian, the 18, that could be my pension if I could get half an idea of what's there, you know what I mean. The rest I'll sell slowly cos I want my money due. If he doesn't deal with you I'll say can I get gold for that. Any shit he doesn't want we will have.'

This certainly gives an intriguing insight into the complex process of offloading criminally procured items without leaving an obvious trail.

The conversation continued.

'Yeah!' Danny's enthusiasm was mounting.

'Yeah, we will have all the shit,' smiled Terry.

Danny was recollecting fast. 'Like last time he threw all them fucking stones away. I put 'em in a big tin, I got a tin like that – that high with, that round,' he gestured a circle shape.

Danny had a stressful memory to share with Terry of almost getting caught out with his precious loot. 'I was round my brother's, I'm in the fucking loft, he lets me go up the loft and turn the light on. Went to get up there, all of a sudden my nephew Paul come in with his girlfriend and is saying what you got up there...? I come back down and they had fucked off.'

Terry and Danny like to contrast their canny demeanour when questioned by the law with Kenny's botched attempt at covert criminality. They had not wanted or expected to get caught but they'd certainly hypothesised about it.

Terry, for example, reminisced about an interrogation on another matter a few years ago. 'He said we got to have an interview. I said not without a solicitor. He said it ain't like that, it's only an interview to tell you what we have nicked you for. I said I don't care, I want a solicitor. So I went in, videod and taped.'

Danny was amused by another recollection. 'Kenny, know it all, breaks into a fucking shoe shop.'

Terry laughed along. 'He could not break into a shoe shop, the cunt don't know the price of anything.'

'No and knows it all,' Danny played along.

'A know-all that knows nothing,' quipped Terry.

'...and one that gets all his gear nicked off him, that's how sharp he is,' smirked Danny.

This kind of exchange once again begs the question of why Kenny was invested in, and entrusted with, such important tasks, but 20/20 hindsight is a wonderful thing.

For all their superior street smarts, it was to be no easier for Terry and Danny than it was for Kenny to mount a defence against the case that would be established against them following the dramatic arrest.

I wanted to find out more about the arrest and the case from someone far better placed to tell me than most, Detective Chief Superintendent Tom Manson.

Tom is a wiry, muscly, striking-looking guy in his early 50s. He has cropped grey hair and searching eyes. Like many police officers who spend enough time chasing gangsters, he could pass for one himself, looks-wise.

I first met Tom in a central London hotel. I had, naturally, done some fact-checking on him first and he is the real deal, a seasoned veteran who appears to be nothing less than the arch enemy of London's organised crime scene. He has been a nightmare for the big north London crime families. Under his responsibility was the Flying Squad, Organised Crime Syndicates, Gun Crime, FALCON (Fraud and Linked Crime ONline) and the Met's kidnap and trafficking divisions. He was described to me in advance of meeting him as 'the quiet man' and 'the guy that actually brought down the Hatton Garden gang'. A lot of people have taken credit publicly, but I have been reliably informed that Tom is the guy that deserves the credit.

I started out by asking him about the prosecution's January 2017 re-assessment of the total value of goods stolen during the raid from £14 million to £25 million – something that could lead to extended prison sentences if the gang do not pay back the money demanded by the courts. I asked whether this is tantamount to a death sentence for each of the men who together have a combined age of several hundred years. His answer surprised me. He explained that he and the Met have no interest in extending their prison sentences. What he wants, he said, is what the public want, to see a photo in the press of these guys having lost everything, standing at the gate of a large, expensive-looking house which is being locked and bolted, carrying only a little holdall. And for that to be made public. It is only if they can't pay the sum that the alternative is sentence extensions. I shudder. Sounds like a nightmare.

I asked him the fundamental question as to whose 'job' it really was. He made the point that although Brian might have co-ordinated the job, when he walked off the job didn't fail. So in that sense he couldn't have been totally in control. He agreed with the idea that there is a split in the group between gangsters and thieves, putting Brian Reader firmly in the violent gangster side of the fence and Danny Jones as a master thief rather than a violent thug.

As I made clear at the beginning of this book, we have been getting this story from Danny and Terry's perspective rather than Brian's, although of course, for all their differences, they also align on many key points.

However, what is certain is that Brian walking off the job turned out to be very useful indeed for the police. Danny, Terry and Basil, as we know, were shocked and furious. Although Danny and Terry stepped up, at times they were slapdash and careless. Under immense pressure, they weren't thinking it all through properly and didn't come up with a new, 'non-Brian' after-plan. Going and buying that second pump in a car that could be traced back to them and signing the documentation as V. Jones... it was all so naïve in Tom's view. They didn't think that the car they were travelling in could be tracked from camera to camera. These old-school thieves literally wouldn't, or couldn't, give sufficient weight to the high-tech reality of the new world they were inhabiting.

CHAPTER TWELVE

THE CASE

*'Forget it, it's over. We are gonna get caught.
It's done.'* (Brian Reader)

The trial took place at Woolwich Crown Court, which is rather ominously located at 2 Belmarsh Road in Thamesmead – right next to HM Prison Belmarsh.

A tunnel links the court to the prison, providing a secure route for bringing defendants in high-profile terrorist cases before the court. Armed police are often deployed to provide additional security.

The Hatton Garden burglary is not the only high-profile case to have been tried at Woolwich. The six men accused of the attempted 21 July 2005 London bombings were tried there in the beginning of 2007. It was also where the men charged with the 2006 transatlantic aircraft plot – involving liquid explosives carried in soft drink containers, which still has an impact on air travel today – were tried.

Before their arrest, Danny and Terry had rehearsed what they would say if they were questioned about the robbery.

Terry said, 'If someone comes to pull you, no comment.'

Danny, planning to pass the buck, said, 'We will go "It's him, it's him!"'

Terry continued, 'No comment, we are arresting you for the Hatton Garden... no comment. I'll say "What, you dopey cunt – I can't even fucking walk." No comment, no comment – pull him for it.'

'We will go, "It's him", agreed Danny. 'It's the first thing you say: "It's bollocks".'

Terry was reminiscing about previous run-ins with the law. 'Like they said to me on the thing 30 years ago. I said, "You what? You're fucking joking ain't ya? The only fucking way I got my money is buying and selling houses, no comment, no comment."'

Danny wasn't convinced by the wisdom of this approach. 'But it's all changed now – [it] goes against you in your defence. But if you know they've got something serious, then you say no comment.'

While not entirely sticking to their guns, there was certainly an element of this tactic at play during the men's trial.

It's worth running formally through the defendants and charges in full for clarity:

- John (Kenny) Collins, 75: pleaded guilty to conspiracy to commit burglary.

- Daniel Jones, 58: pleaded guilty to conspiracy to commit burglary.

- Terry Perkins, 67: pleaded guilty to conspiracy to commit burglary.

- Brian Reader, 76: pleaded guilty to conspiracy to commit burglary.

- Carl Wood, 58: Charged with conspiracy to commit burglary and conspiracy to conceal, convert or transfer criminal property.

- William (Billy) Lincoln, 60: Charged with conspiracy to commit burglary and conspiracy to conceal, convert or transfer criminal property

- Jon Harbinson, 42: Charged with conspiracy to commit burglary and conspiracy to conceal, convert or transfer criminal property.

- Hugh Doyle, 48: Charged with conspiracy to conceal, convert or transfer criminal property and faced an alternative charge of concealing, converting or transferring criminal property.

There was to be plenty of theatre in court during the trial, and some unexpected moments of levity and even hilarity.

Absurdly, Hugh Doyle couldn't resist tweeting his followers on his way to court, posting a picture of his company car next to the text: 'On Woolwich ferry on way to court, last day of 37 days in court, hope let's hope I don't have to walk the plank!!'

He then added: 'Forget A rated prison – have you got a G rated boiler? £400 cash back for new boiler.'

It is difficult not to marvel at his bid to turn his trial into a marketing opportunity.

THE CASE

One of the best moments came when Danny Jones offered to reveal where he had stashed some of the loot. On 24 November 2015, Martin Evans, crime correspondent for *The Daily Telegraph*, recounted that:

'One of the ringleaders of the Hatton Garden jewellery heist buried his stash in the cemetery plots of two relatives but only revealed one of them to the police.

'Daniel Jones, 58, who admitted his part in the country's biggest ever burglary, offered to tell detectives where he had hidden his share of the £14 million worth of jewellery, gems and gold following his arrest. He told officers he had buried the items in a memorial plot at Edmonton Cemetery in north London, belonging to a male relative of his partner, and said if he was taken from prison he could show them exactly where it was hidden.

'But before taking him up on his offer, suspicious officers from Scotland Yard's Flying Squad, searched the area themselves and found a large stash hidden under the memorial stone of his father-in-law. A short time later, Jones was taken from prison and led police to the first plot where a smaller stash of jewellery was hidden.

'Details of Jones's attempt to dupe the police emerged

on the second day of the Hatton Garden trial, where four men are facing charges of conspiracy to burgle and launder the proceeds of the crime. Philip Evans, prosecuting, told the jury at Woolwich Crown Court, said: "Following his plea of guilty to the conspiracy to burgle one of the defendants, Mr Jones, offered to take the police to the place where he had buried some of the proceeds from this crime and which were part of his share. Whilst arrangements were being put in place for that to happen, the police conducted their own investigations to see whether they could find Mr Jones 'stash' before they took Mr Jones to show them."

'Mr Evans explained how detectives established that one of the plots in Edmonton cemetery bore the name of a man called Sidney James Hart, who was the father of his partner, Valerie Hart.

'He went on: "Having obtained permission to do so the police searched the memorial site by digging up the ground under the memorial stone. There were two bags, one blue, which was sealed with tape and one red, orange and white, which contained a large quantity of jewellery.

"One week later on the 15th October the police did take Mr Jones out of prison so that he could show them where the jewellery was hidden. He was not told of the earlier find. Mr Jones directed the police, perhaps unsurprisingly, to the same cemetery in Edmonton. He then identified an area of the cemetery and a memorial stone. This memorial stone was however for a man named Sidney John Hart, who may also be another relation of Valerie Hart, the mother of Daniel Jones' children.

"Underneath the memorial stone Mr Jones revealed what appeared to be a black and orange bag. That bag has now been opened and found to contain various items of gold and jewellery and a much smaller number of packets or Brifkas containing precious stones.

'Mr Jones then told the police that he was the only person who knew it was there, and, importantly, he said, "There's no other outstanding property. That is all I had."

'He was then specifically asked whether there was anywhere else the police needed to go in order to recover property, and he replied, "That's all I had. The rest of it you got on the day". Mr Jones was then returned to the prison.

Mr Evans said Jones had not told police about the existence of the larger stash because he wanted to keep it for his "future use".' Good old Danny. Always playing games!

Judge Christopher Kinch was damning, though, in his remarks during sentencing, and wanted to make it clear that he had no intention granting leniency to the robbers on account of their age: 'Far from stumbling into 21st century crime as relics of a past era, the conspirators were clearly highly aware of the dangers of leaving traces that could lead to their identification,' he said.

Explaining his decision to disregard the sentencing guidelines, the judge said the case involved greater harm than those covered by the guidelines. 'The theft and damage inevitably caused significant financial and economic loss on an unprecedented scale. The consequences for the company and for some of the individual jewellers were serious indeed. The safety deposit company went into administration, its reputation in ruins and it no longer operates as it did.

'Many of the losers were small independent jewellers,' the judge said, including those who were keeping stock for their retirement. 'In my judgment it must rank among the worst offences of its type... It would be contrary to the interests of justice to follow the definitive guideline, which was simply not designed with a case of this scale in mind.'

Danny, Terry and Kenny, faced with all the police

surveillance footage and recordings, had been forced to admit it was a fair cop during the trial.

At sentencing, they were muted and deferential. When the judge handed down the sentences, Danny simply said, 'Thank you, judge.'

Terry reacted with a 'Thank you, sir.'

In order to get a handle on exactly what the case against the Hatton Garden gang was, I needed the best legal brain I had encountered in my career. What I wanted was a deep dive into the legal implications of the case with Jeremy Dein, one of our most prominent and high-profile QCs. Jeremy has been a QC since 2003 and is the country's leading criminal defence counsel. He is the joint head of chambers, and head of the Crime Group, at 25 Bedford Row.

Jeremy's real forte is serious crime, in particular murder. No one in recent years has defended more murder cases at the Old Bailey, including some of the most headline-hitting cases in modern history, from the 'shopping trolley killer' to honour killings in Pakistan. He also represented a senior police officer at the Hillsborough inquest.

Jeremy and I became good mates not on a murder trial but during his astonishing defence for former NDubz star and X Factor judge, Tulisa Contostavlos.

This trial ended in the first ever stay of proceedings in an entrapment case.

I loved watching Jeremy work, a combination of brains, passion, kindness and pure theatre. He's in serious demand on the TV and radio when he's not in court. In person and outside of the formal legal garb, he's shy and a notably trendy dresser.

Jeremy had plenty of cogent thoughts about why this case had created, relatively anyway, such sympathy and good feeling towards these 'Diamond Geezers' or "Diamond Wheezers" as they have become known.

My first big question for Jeremy was focused around media attention. I wanted to know, what is it like to be defending such a high-profile case, one that attracts considerable publicity? Jeremy gave me a lucid, frank and considered response:

'The truth is that for any individual charged with a criminal offence, the situation is incredibly stressful. It's not until a person becomes embroiled in the system that all the anxieties involved become apparent.'

I wanted to know how it felt defending in a case where, once the trial has begun, publicity absolutely reigns on a daily basis. Jeremy was certainly a highly seasoned player in this regard. As he said:

'Media attention creates pressures, whatever the

nature of the case. The need to check publicity and make sure it is accurate, and not over-sensationalised, creates added pressures... Frankly, defence counsel can do without this because the complications on mounting a defence are generally huge enough in themselves... I also have concerns so far as the jury are concerned in cases where media publicity characterises the trial daily. The suggestion that the jury are not influenced by sensational headlines, or the like, is unrealistic. Of course, juries these days are prohibited from accessing the internet in terms of researching the case. Very strict judicial directions are given on this – and that's a good thing.

'Whether those directions are complied with is another matter...' he added, wryly.

Jeremy continued, 'The kind of judges who are allocated high-profile cases do not feel they have to pander to the media – they simply want to do the right thing. We should all be grateful for this aspect of the criminal justice process, it's vital – trial by jury, trial by evidence, and trouble in media is not what we need. Largely, that is what happens with the local justice process. Long may it continue.'

Leading on from these hugely helpful observations, I wanted to know how Jeremy perceived the role of public opinion in its interaction with an extraordinary case such as this one. He found it just as intriguing as I did:

'It is fascinating. Of course the public are largely against crime, especially serious crime. On the whole, members of the public deprecate the commission of criminal offences and want to see those involved punished. However, my experience is that in cases such as this, there is, perversely, sometimes an underlying feeling of adulation – even admiration. I sense this from talking to people and from a climate when a case such as this is subject to trial and inevitable publicity.'

Leading on from this, Jeremy crystallised the features of the Hatton Garden safe deposit burglary that drew this response from the public and gave the case an element of romance.

* The fact that the burglary was well planned and carried out by elderly men, albeit experienced villains
* The fact that the burglary occurred during the Easter bank holiday and Passover
* The mystery of press reports speculating that the major underground fire at Holborn station was started as a diversion

THE CASE

* The challenging manner in which entry was made – the suggestion that the burglars had abseiled down a lift shaft, then driven through thick walls with a power drill

I was also very keen to hear Jeremy's perspective as one of the UK's most seasoned QCs on the sentences meted out to the gang. He told me that the aggravating factors that led to the gang's long sentences included:

* The fact that the burglary required careful, detailed and intense planning.
* Once inside the building, a key element in breaching security was the identification of the lift shaft as a means of securing entry to the basement.
* The successful penetration of the vault required detailed knowledge of the building, its security systems and weak points.
* The hard drives to the CCTV systems for the building and the vault were removed.
* The conspirators had brought with them equipment to cut alarm wires.
* The estimate of the total value of the stolen property was just short of £14 million, although this was later revised by the prosecution to closer to £25 million.

* The professionalism of a crime is a major factor. It is difficult for defence counsel to argue against a very long sentence where such professionalism has set in.

Jeremy continued: 'Obviously, as a defence barrister, I find myself asking the fundamental question of why people are behaving this way? In my view the defendants who committed this offence offer fascinating examples of the criminal mindset – the truth is they are not violent but ingenious. There are seven long sentences because of the gravity of the offence, but they are not a danger to the public as I perceive it.

In truth, it probably doesn't matter how long their sentences are. Prison is an occupational hazard.'

On reflection, Jeremy's brilliant mind came up with further, controversial thoughts around the sentencing of these robbers vis-à-vis other sentences handed down in the UK justice system. I sat down with him to talk it out in one of his favourite north London haunts. As our drinks arrived he started animatedly talking about his specialist subject – crime and punishment.

'The sentence for a one-punch manslaughter is maybe four years, possibly five. These guys got seven. How do we work out what crime deserves what punishment? How have we arrived at a position where taking a life can sometimes attract a lesser sentence than sophisticated crimes such as the Hatton Garden robberies?'

He fell silent and thought for a moment before going on.

'So, are jewels more valuable than life? It doesn't really make sense. And then when these two criminals get to prison, the one-punch killer and the sophisticated robber, they might end up sharing a cell together. There is no rhyme or reason to it.'

Blimey, I thought. If an eminent QC can come to that position, what hope is there for the rest of us?

Something very significant indeed for the case suddenly hit before the Christmas decorations were down in January 2016, eight months after the robbery. News broke that a fabulously wealthy woman, and she would have to be, had only just noticed that £7 million of her gold had gone missing from the vault. She claimed she had only discovered the bullion was missing after the six gang members went on trial. If the loss was confirmed, it would take the stated value of the whole haul up to a staggering £21 million.

Scotland Yard issued a statement confirming that her claim was received in June 2016.

Jon and Val could not have been more sceptical about this claim when we first caught up about it in 2017. Nursing his shandy, Jon chuckled as Val got animated talking about just how fishy it was that this woman had waited this long to come forward. She found the timing of the revelation of the claim by Scotland Yard suddenly just a week before the gang's POCA hearing 'very bloody convenient'.

The £7 million in gold equates to 215kg, which is more than could fit into one of those little deposit boxes. Plus there is no reference in the transcripts of the gang's conversations to all that gold... and there would be. There is so much confusion about what is worth what, but all of them would know the value of a gold bar.

There had to be more to this than meets the eye. One thing that really came across to me in all my conversations with the gang and their associates is the idea that this robbery 'embarrassed the establishment' and they were being made examples of as a result. They felt that there were orders coming down to the police from 'on high' to throw the book at our gang and to do everything necessary. It was a theory I didn't fully understand, but it was repeated to me again and again. That judges, politicians and top businessmen had boxes in the vault that had been hit, and for them, the 'establishment', this was personal. You make up your own minds as to whether you think this is true, but the gang members will believe it until their dying breaths.

On 31 January 2017, there was another, shattering, development. The value of the goods stolen in the Hatton Garden jewellery raid had risen to an estimated £25million. It was originally thought the value of the items stolen over the 2015 Easter holiday was £14million. However, prosecutors were now seeking the larger sum from the five 'ringleaders' convicted of the robbery. If they do not pay back the sum each gang member would face a maximum of 14 years added to their sentences without parole.

The full confiscation hearing – set to begin in January 2018 – is expected to last around six weeks.

It's worth explaining a little bit about the Proceeds of Crime Act 2002 (POCA), as it is this legislation that allows such a development in the case to occur. POCA became law on 24 July 2002 and was established as a means of ensuring that criminals found guilty of a crime could not benefit financially from that crime. The Act allows for the proceeds of crime to be retrieved via a confiscation order, which requires a convicted defendant to pay the State a specified sum of money by a specified date. That date has to be no later than six months after the date on which the order is made.

It's up to the Crown Court to work out both the benefit obtained by the defendant (in this case how much they stole during the robbery) and the defendant's available amount. Then the confiscation order uses whichever is the smaller of these two figures to come up with the recoverable amount. The defendant's available amount is typically the market value of all his or her assets minus the amount of any liabilities which are secured upon those assets.

This whole concept of POCA is a fairly recent innovation and certainly not something our diamond wheezers grew up with. To cut a long story short, for the Hatton Garden gang, it could spell total financial ruin. And if they couldn't come up with the money, it would lead to a much longer prison sentence. This whole situation made monitoring the criminal case almost as exciting as watching the robbers' story unfurl in their own words.

POCA in this case, and indeed generally, is a dogfight with the solicitors on the side of the villains pushing the figure down and the police and CPS pushing the figure up. The burden of proof falls to the police and CPS to demonstrate actual values and losses, to arrive at some sort of meaningful figure. This game of slowly, slowly catchy monkey shines a torch on the lives led by these villains, either chasing loot or running from the law.

POCA has had another effect too, upon the creative industries, presumably one that the police did not anticipate. As a TV producer, a lot of the time I am out talking to people and trying to get them to tell me their stories. And since POCA has come into force it is now so much more difficult to get the criminal fraternity to talk to producers or authors, because no financial incentive can be provided to them, or even to their often completely blameless spouses and families.

The other negative effect of POCA in this context has been to make villains incredibly wary about telling stories of their dim and distant pasts. It has made them intensely fearful of a knock on the door and an investigation into how they came to buy that house back in 1985, that sports car and so on. Very few villains would welcome that kind of lifestyle audit.

CHAPTER THIRTEEN

THE PRISON

'Anyone who grassed me like that, you know what I would say… He was with us.' (Terry Perkins)

While on remand awaiting trial, and then again after sentencing, the gang ended up in the outer reaches of south-east London, at HM Prison Belmarsh. One of Britain's most notorious high-security prisons, it is no stranger to 'celebrity guests'. In addition to the Hatton Garden gang, Belmarsh has also been home for a very colourful array of characters, past and present. Jeffrey Archer spent a few weeks there and later wrote about his experiences (of course). Abu Hamza, aka

'Captain Hook', the extremist cleric who lost his hand in an explosion, was in Belmarsh before his extradition to the US. The media was amused to find that he complained bitterly about his time there.

Waheed Zaman, who plotted to blow up a transatlantic flight in 2006, did time there, as did the 21/7 bombers and Bilal Abdullah, mastermind of the botched Glasgow Airport terrorist attack. Perhaps the most famous resident of all was Charles Bronson, once deemed Britain's most violent criminal. Memorably portrayed onscreen in a star-making turn by Tom Hardy, he used to have an entire wing of the Belmarsh High Security Unit (HSU) all to himself. The HSU, a concrete building without windows, was built in 1991 primarily to house IRA prisoners.

Infamous British gangster Curtis Warren is serving a long sentence at Belmarsh for drug smuggling. Interestingly in the context of the gang, in November 2013 Warren was ordered to pay a £198 million confiscation order, or face another decade in jail. In March 2014 the news broke that Warren had lost his appeal over his failure to pay the order, and so he would remain in Belmarsh, where he still is today.

The gang told me that they were kept in the Category A section of Belmarsh for four months in a small section that they called 'the Unit' while they awaited trial. They were allowed no calls and no visits. They spent 23 hours a day in the cell, with just one hour's exercise in the yard. The light in their cell was turned on for two minutes every hour, disrupting their already fitful sleep. It is as tough as jail gets in this country, but was it a problem for these hardened thieves?

In a word, yes. Every single one of them was feeling the pressure. These are old men, and not just that. They have lived hard lives and done hard time. In addition to the very real hardship of years in Belmarsh, there was a lurking fear given their age, which Danny and Terry articulated to one another in their darkest moments: Was this going to turn out to be a death sentence?

This wasn't necessarily the only complication of a long stay in Belmarsh, either. There has been unhelpful nonsense talk of the Adams family (a notorious London crime family) having beef with the gang, but they state categorically that this is not true. More to the point, Patsy Adams was on 'the Unit' at Belmarsh with them when they were first remanded in custody and there were no issues with him.

Belmarsh's HSU is a prison-within-a-prison. There

are 843 prisoners in the main jail and only nine in HSU, a bespoke facility for the UK's most dangerous criminals. It reminds me of my time filming inside Broadmoor. While the HSU houses some of Britain's most hardened and dangerous criminals, the main prison is a more provincial affair with local men serving short-term sentences.

Entry to the main prison at Belmarsh is via 15 different gated doors. You have to have your fingerprints scanned to gain access.

In the main prison, inmates are allowed to do various forms of menial labour like cleaning, but in HSU no one is allowed to work. It's just too risky to supervise them and besides, they are rarely out of their cells, whereas prisoners in the main prison spend half their time outside them. After a quick breakfast just after 8am they're allowed to exercise outside and use the gym. They have to clean up for a bit but then they can watch telly, hang out, or go back to the gym again. Belmarsh is pretty short-staffed, so any activity that the prisoners can undertake is informed by this fact.

Danny did take one little trip out of Belmarsh. The date was 15 October 2015 and the destination was Edmonton cemetery.

The purpose of the trip was for him to take the

officers to the place, or places, where had said he'd hidden the stolen goods. Danny had expressed willingness to comply with the police in showing where he had hidden some bags. On a thrilling trip out of Belmarsh under a jittery police escort, he changed cars five times and there was a huge motorcade and helicopters above.

The day *before* the robbery Danny asked Val if she had a 'Bag for Life'. She didn't know what it was for, but it turned out that, when the police dug up the gravestones, the loot was buried in this Bag for Life. The graves where the loot was buried belonged to Val's mum, dad and brother. Danny was really worried Val would be cross with him if it emerged that he had put some of his stash under her relative's grave and used the Bag for Life he had borrowed from her a few days earlier.

Danny was cheerfully oblivious to what the police had already found in the cemetery. He took the police to a second plot in the same cemetery where he had buried a smaller stash under the memorial stone of another one of his relatives. I would have loved to be a fly on the wall for this entire episode, and it must have presented an utterly bizarre spectacle to any mourners going about their business that day.

On one of her 2016 visits to Belmarsh, Val abruptly walked straight past Brian Reader in the corridor. She said just the sight of him made her catch her breath. 'He looked so ill. Really, really ill. I couldn't believe the change in him.' Once a cool-looking hale and hearty older chap, advancing years, prostate cancer recovery and strokes, and the rigours of incarceration had taken a fearful toll on Brian. He was a frail and broken man.

When Val visits Danny in Belmarsh, she is well aware that they have lip readers, cameras, everything to try and listen and learn as much as possible from each visit. Danny plays up to this and has fun elaborately winking and tapping his fingers in a made-up pattern to try and confuse the guards and amuse himself.

Val has to assume, though, that everything she says and writes to Danny is the subject of surveillance. She says she knows that a number of her letters to him have simply gone missing. In many ways, Val and Danny are deeply personal, protective of their privacy. Val describes herself as shy.

Val has been upset by some of the quirkier nuggets about Danny that have come out. Carl Wood took the opportunity to humiliate Danny during the trial on a number of counts, including his assertions that Danny was 'eccentric to extremes that everyone who knew Danny would say he was mad. He would go to bed in his mother's dressing gown with a fez on. He would read palms, tell people he could read their fortunes – bit of a Walter Mitty.'

The 'dressing gown' was actually Val's mum's. It's true that he used to like to wear it. He loved her mum. The fez hat thing was completely made up. Carl also made reference to Danny speaking to Rocket, his white-haired terrier, as if it was human. Danny loves to talk to dogs and has long conversations with the dog. Val and Danny see no shame in that.

I have some form on prison investigations myself, which maybe on some level granted me some important empathy, or at least a genuine curiosity, with the kind of environments in which Danny and Kenny have spent far too much of their adult lives and, indeed, old age.

I have always been fascinated by serious and organised crime and by the men and women who engage in it. For one reason or another, I became particularly obsessed with Broadmoor, the most secure of high security hospitals. I set myself a pressing personal challenge to see if I could get inside.

I first walked through the gates in 2006 when I made a documentary about madness and creativity. One of the psychiatrists was even able to exclusively show me art works made by the patients. Some of it was haunting and evocative, and much of the art was highly skilled and intricate. They wouldn't let me film inside the wards, only in the visitors' centre. I was determined to gain access to the wards and tell the never-before-told stories from inside, both from patient and staff perspectives.

Broadmoor fascinates me more than almost anywhere. It is full of highly disturbed psychopaths, cannibals, child murderers, arsonists and serial killers. But they are patients not prisoners. They are at a high-security hospital ultimately because they are acutely unwell and require that combination of care, treatment and security. As the months and years passed I looked into their eyes and talked to them as people, sat next to them drinking cups of tea, watched them work in the metal and woodwork centres and visited their bedrooms and communal areas. After months and months of visits it became the new normal to me, and the patients would sometimes talk openly to me about what they had done, often in denial about the seriousness of their crimes, other times telling me accounts of their appalling childhoods, stories of horrifying sexual and physical abuse. Sometimes their stories sickened me, and when I left the hospital at the end of the day I would have vivid images in my head of some of the things they had told me. After five years of visits and a further year of filming, I had enjoyed extraordinary access to this unique institution. I have the utmost respect for the bravery, professionalism and commitment of the staff at Broadmoor and their astonishing achievements and research.

The prison hardships for all the men came up at the trial, too. Carl Wood's defence lawyer Nick Corsellis eloquently described the tribulations of his client. He pointed out to the judge that Carl's jail term meant he would 'not see' his elderly and sickly parents again. The prisoners' remand in the HSU was 'particularly difficult' because it meant just one hour of exercise a day and even that, according to Nick Corsellis, 'is very rare that that is achieved – half an hour at best. Half an hour of daylight.' Nick indicated that Carl's mental health had been affected by the remand in custody, which he found so 'difficult to bear'.

Danny and Terry have suffered in equal measure. Danny is also keenly aware of what he perceives to be the injustice of his situation, highlighting the sort of prisoner he finds himself next to. As he wrote in a letter to Sky crime correspondent Martin Brunt after his incarceration for the Hatton Garden robbery, 'They took that sex killer Levi Belfour [sic – it is Bellfield] a few years ago, he showed the police where he killed those women. So, there you go, Martin, a sex killer and there's me, a 58-year-old burnt-out burglar. Maybe they think I'm going to get [a] hit squad to get me out, my God how stupid.'

In addition to what he justifiably viewed as this injustice, he was also concerned about the treatment he was receiving from the authorities in his letters to Brunt, bearing out the sense of victimisation I have also noted in my conversations with other gang members. Danny wrote, 'They are trying to make me look a bad person. I'm trying my best to put things right and for some reason they don't want me to give it back.' As he also reflected, with genuine bewilderment, 'You would have thought the police would have jumped with joy, but for some reason which I don't know, they are not that interested.'

Something I have already indicated that I found really compelling from day one is the advanced age of the dependants, and the implications of that for their imprisonment. Jeremy Dein QC had some fascinating and very humane reflections for me when I asked him about it.

'There is always something slightly strange about representing older defendants. To me, the criminal justice process is designed for younger people. This is not a rational feeling, but one that tends to stick with me. Of course, if elderly defendants – such as these men – commit serious offences, the need for prosecution, trial and sentence, remains. I'm not in any way suggesting that this ought not to apply. However, as a criminal defence barrister, I suggest that the concept of imprisonment is that much more difficult and challenging. To be incarcerated in your 60s or 70s must be physically very difficult, and to be surrounded by younger people in similar circumstances, must be an unpleasant, if not bizarre experience. I have little doubt that the same applies the other way round. I have had young defendants tell me that it's strange to be locked up with people of their dad or even granddad's age. Not surprising perhaps.

'It was inevitable that the defendants in the Hatton Garden burglary case were made subject to prosecution, trial and punishment. What makes offenders of this age continue to want to subject themselves to the arduous process of criminal proceedings, it is fascinating. As I have said, in one sense, the age of the offenders added glamour and curiosity to the case. But then, however much they put on a brave face, make no mistake, it must be very tough, especially when long sentences are handed out – an occupational hazard, perhaps, but still an incredibly tough experience starting a long sentence when you are an old age pensioner.'

I wanted to thrash out the issue of threat with Jeremy, too. The decision to put these old criminals in the HSU for any length of time felt like a controversial one to me. I don't want to diminish how grave their crimes had been. But did they really pose a threat to society at large? To the same extent as the terrorists and drug dealers they had been on the HSU with? It was basically the same point Danny had made about not exactly being Levi Bellfield.

Jeremy agreed, and said he wondered how much the average citizen really cares these days about locking up the Hatton Garden robbers. These old-fashioned villains are generally cooperative and polite. They are respectful of the system if not happy to go inside – they respect the judge if not the sentence given. It's those who do not respect the system that present bigger issues by way of threat to society, those who want to destroy us. The issues are very complex.

THE PRISON

On several of my meetings in Enfield I talked with Val and Jon about a prison visit for me to see Danny and Terry, and how it could best work. He could have two visits a week, and a Sunday visit could be a double visit. The plan was for me to take one of Danny's visits and for Terry to have a visit at the same time. A further important component of the plan was that the two of them would sit next to each other. That way, I could chat to Danny and also have a quick conversation with Terry. It all sounded good to me.

They warned me just how long it takes to get all the way out to Belmarsh and how early I would have to set off. I was happy either way, whether it be a Wednesday or a Sunday, whatever suited. Jon and Val suggested that we have me down as a friend of the family when we go as not to arouse any suspicion. Danny had agreed. I would not take a notepad and we would just chat. I was completely up for it and looking forward to finally meeting Danny and Terry. We chose dates and then they cancelled. New dates and they cancelled again. I started to get worried. Something must be up. I left it for a few weeks and then brought it up again at my next face-to-face with Val and Jon. It wasn't going to happen. There were too many factors at play.

CHAPTER FOURTEEN
MORE DRAMA

'It's not been easy. I've got things in here too [points at head] that I'd rather weren't there. Oh, aye. I can keep them at bay, yeah. But they're waiting for me.'
(Albert Pierrepoint, as written by Jeff Pope)

With the hangover fading from the New Year celebrations, activity had started thick and fast in 2017.

Meanwhile, back on the outside, Jeff Pope and Terry Winsor were powering on with the drama, which was really coming together even while things were falling apart at the seams again for the gang.

Jeff and Terry had not only been working away at the timeline but were moving towards starting a first draft of their script. They had question after question for me, and I was doing my best to answer them as accurately as I could using every single one of my contacts in the underworld.

Filming was well underway on the first low-budget, quick-turnaround movie, too: *The Hatton Garden Job*. This story just kept getting bigger and bigger. Capitalising on both the crime's status as the biggest burglary in British legal history and on the advanced years of the perpetrators, a British-made film intended to tell this very British story. It was directed by Ronnie Thompson; Larry Lamb, a staple of British working-class hero character acting, was slightly miscast as Brian Reader. The film made some peculiar decisions in the plot and narrative, too.

Basil was presented as a career thief who was persuaded to join the Hatton Garden gang just days after finishing a custodial sentence for another crime. Hired thug mercenaries and the Hungarian mafia made strange appearances in the story.

As always, journalists covering this film adaptation picked up on the age of the men involved, and the old-school nature of their crime. The film was released in the UK on 14 April 2017 to rather poor reviews. Quickly put together and miles from the truth, it felt opportunistic and inauthentic.

Another film, this time with more high-profile names attached to it, was also in the works, made by the highly credible powerhouse production company Working Title. If the press around this film was to be believed then some of Britain's most venerable actors-of-a-certain-age had been lured into the project, including Michael Caine, Ray Winstone, Jim Broadbent and Michael Gambon. Michael Caine was to be cast as Brian Reader. Caine had gone on record expressing enthusiasm for the project, based on his fascination with the 'very, very tough' gang, a fascination he shared with Ray Winstone. According to Caine he would 'do it in an instant'. Working Title's glossier, bigger-budget take on the story is being directed by the highly regarded James Marsh. James had earned his reputation on solid, important and well-received movies, including *Man on Wire* and *The Theory of Everything*.

Bizarrely, it looked from some of these media stories that started to run in spring 2016 that a third movie – *The Hatton Garden Heist* – was being made by Fulwell Pictures. This would have provided me with another close personal connection to the Hatton Garden robbery. However, it materialised the film wasn't going ahead, but it did show yet again what an enduring public interest there was in any version of the retelling of this gripping story.

Excitement and buzz aside however, some of Jeff and Terry's questions were hard to ask, let alone answer. Why exactly was I doing this again I thought.

It was time for another meeting with Danny's common-law wife Val, too. I felt that familiar blend of excitement and unease. It wasn't easy getting all the information I needed for the story; I was under pressure for more revelations and there were times with some of the villains when it didn't feel safe. What price was I willing to pay to get the story out there?

The first half of January 2017 was doom and gloom for both the gang themselves and for the whole London criminal fraternity, with the proceeds of crime hearings starting badly.

On a grim, drizzly January Monday afternoon, with a Tube strike in full force, Emma and I made our way back to the Crews Hill pub for another meeting with Val and Jon. Emma and I were a bit early and everyone entering the pub 'looked the part'. We smiled in misguided recognition a couple of times before our real companions arrived. Sting was playing in the background and various punters studied the *Daily Star* racing pages. The sturdy oak beams, ketchup bottles and cutlery in baskets, punters bustling in from the garden centre sales, and country cider on tap all communicated a slightly old-fashioned form of Englishness.

We sat on one side of the bar all together. Two couples having an afternoon drink. Nothing suspicious about that. However, once we started talking, I was glad no one appeared to be within earshot. What they shared with me that day, in what I reckon was the most exciting of the many meetings that I had, has been carefully dispersed throughout this book. Finally, I had the answers to some of the issues that had been bothering me the most.

January 2017 had also seen the death of Lenny (or Lennie) Gibson, another 'gentleman thief', if you will. Lenny had been involved in the Silver Bullion Robbery on 24 March 1980. Several of my key contacts were at this funeral and they had taken the news of his death hard.

As one villain said to me, 'It was a massive funeral. Lenny Gibson, big time robber. Google his name: Silver bullion robbery!!! Very respected man. He fought cancer for 9 years, brave man.' It sounded like Lennie had been given an old-school send-off. Whatever you think about these guys, I had to smile to myself about their loyalty and respect for each other to the end.

It was easy to see that such deaths, combined with the constant hovering anxiety that their own prison terms, already tough, would be extended, was taking its toll on the gang. Would they die in prison? Had their luck run out? So far they had been given fairly short sentences, and public opinion seemed to be on their side. However, looking out at the rain beating down on the leafless trees of Enfield, it felt like maybe the pendulum was shifting. Sitting opposite Tom Manson at St Pancras station as he explained to me the incredible success of the Proceeds of Crime Act, it had felt like the power balance had finally shifted. The police were winning. And even though I am law abiding, something about that made me feel a bit glum.

CHAPTER FIFTEEN

WHERE'S BASIL?

'He will never get nicked in a million years.'
(Danny Jones)

That particularly fascinating one of my meetings with Jon and Val, plus my discussions with senior policemen, had prompted me to revisit in depth what I *did* know about Basil. Neither the gang, nor the police, nor my other underworld contacts want to make my job easy on this topic. Even so, I had made some extraordinary discoveries.

The police officially tended to imply that Basil was an outsider. Difficult to pin down and very much outside the gang in many ways. I am not so sure. And I think they have put that out as a line as opposed to something they genuinely believe themselves. As I bring this book to a close, I strongly believe that the police now know who Basil is. However, I don't believe they know where he is. We know he is, or at least was, abroad, perhaps inspired by the words of Arthur Daley, 'You can't find a good honest-to-God decent professional thief anymore, they've all gone to live in bloody Spain.'

The police dedicated huge resources to searching through ANPR footage and CCTV and I believe they had a breakthrough, have figured out who he is and are working with INTERPOL and the foreign intelligence services to track Basil down overseas. During research for the drama, Jeff Pope and Terry Winsor had spoken to sources who suggested his destination could have been Panama.

It didn't take long after the news of the heist broke for the rumour to begin to circulate that Basil was a former policeman himself, and therefore the subject of a police cover-up. Certainly there are many reasons why the police might want to keep that information quiet, even if just for the time being. Having been through the transcripts with a fine toothcomb many times, there are certain places where Basil is mentioned and the police lose audio at exactly that point.

For instance, as part of a lengthy recording taken in mid-May 2015, Danny and Terry were talking about how no one would believe some of the astonishing aspects of the robbery and their involvement.

Danny said, 'Oh my good God, fuck me, do you know what we used to call the book? Billy Liar.'

Terry then agreed and jumped in with, 'They would never believe it, would they? Look at this cunt, who the fuck is he? Mr Bean, that's what.'

Then there is a one-minute long section in the transcripts that is missed out and marked 'equipment adjustment' twice.

When this 'equipment adjustment' is complete, the audio picks up on Terry saying to Danny 'similar age to your age I said… Carl, I looked at him and thought I'm fucking different.' Danny and Terry can surely only have been talking about Basil at this point, before moving on to chat about Carl.

Another extremely suspicious 'equipment adjustment' later in the same conversation came immediately after Danny and Terry had dismissed Basil as a 'cunt bollocks' because he had persuaded Kenny to suggest to Terry that he store Basil's gear,

'He said well you might as well keep Basil's there, I'll keep Basil's here,' and Terry had angrily asked Danny, 'You ever seen a shambles like it, fucking cunts, cunts.' Then between 10.10 and 10.12pm, there are three 'equipment adjustments' before the audio returns in time for an anodyne discussion about marginal character Terry Bailey. Having completely lost sound during a highly incriminating discussion of what and where Basil was storing in terms of loot. Pretty convenient, huh?

Even more extraordinary, though, is something that takes place in a three-way conversation between Danny, Terry and Kenny. The conversation had started with a straightforward critique of Brian for abandoning the job.

Danny commenced, saying, 'And all them months and fucking years he put the work in, just to go "look, I won't be here tomorrow". Cos he's thought them cunts, you'll never get in there and the simplest fucking thing, common sense thing got you in.'

Terry was in full agreement. 'He's a fucking idiot by doing that… I'll tell you, all I could say is…'

Kenny also concurred, pointing out that 'Saying that, common sense tells ya, that he never thought we would get in.'

'No, he didn't,' agrees Danny.

Then here comes the critical bit. The beginning of Kenny's response to Danny is marked as '(INAUDIBLE)'. When the audio ostensibly picks up again, Kenny is noted as saying, 'There's only one thing that you'd give that up for, one reason ever, you must have thought that we would never get its [sic], the only reason you wouldn't come back innit.'

It is impossible not to surmise that in the 'inaudible' bit, Kenny was talking about the mysterious thing that Basil went in for, the Holy Grail which no one will disclose and which affected everyone's motivations.

It is quite striking how often things go inaudible when Basil is the conversation topic. At another crucial moment discussing why Basil let the alarm go off, Terry says, 'Well, I think he made a rip there (inaudible) lucky.' Lucky how? Because he was an ex-policeman? Because it was an inside job?

Tellingly, page 36 of the transcripts is missing altogether. It is intriguingly preceded by a three-way discussion between Terry, Danny and Kenny about logistics.

After a portion of Danny's conversation marked 'inaudible', Kenny simply says, 'Tuesday.'

Danny corrects him, saying, 'No, you said pop over Monday to make arrangements.'

Kenny swiftly replies, 'Yes yes yes, sorry, yes, I'll find something just to take that', then it is marked 'inaudible'.

Danny's response is also initially marked inaudible, until the innocuous logistics of '...alright, half ten, eleven.'

Once again, the next part of Kenny's response is marked 'inaudible, then he says '...all done then, you're talking about Monday.'

Danny agrees. Kenny replies, 'Whatever.' Terry chimes in with a confirmatory 'Half ten, eleven.'

Then there is an entire comment by Danny marked 'inaudible'.

Kenny is then quoted simply saying, 'Whatever, whatever, OK.' Then comes the entire missing page, which contains the rest of this conversation, because when the transcripts pick up again, it is a new recording from the evening of 16 May 2015.

So, while on the one hand it seems certain that there will come a point when he gets caught, that need never happen if Basil is under some form of police protection or embargo. I keep revisiting what Danny had said about Basil. That he would 'Never get nicked in a million years.' Well, not if the police already know who he is, he won't. Is that why the gang say he'll never get caught?

There is a clue to Basil and his identity in the covert police recordings – at one point Danny is quoted as saying 'Basil will have to come all the way back over' – the implication being that he lives abroad.

Danny, Terry, Jon, Val and all of my underworld sources are completely and understandably silent on Basil, but it is obvious from the police transcripts that Danny knew Basil pretty well by the end of the job. After all, it was always going to be Basil who went through the hole into the vault with Danny. It was Danny and Basil who actually did the job of breaking open and emptying the boxes.

We know that Basil was certainly the youngest of the gang by quite a stretch. He seems from various clues to be a trained electrician. If he wasn't in on the plan from the very beginning, and I think that he was, he was certainly in on it from the moment that they decided to use a drill. He was, in other words, at the heart of the gang with Danny, not a marginal, shadowy element of it. The fact he has been a shadow *since* the job doesn't change that. I have exclusively revealed that Basil was Reader's man. And that it was Brian Reader that brought Basil onto the job in the first place.

Basil's technical know-how has been well documented. He had thought ahead and taken out the hard drives from the CCTV. All the footage from Greville Street shows a man who knew exactly where all the cameras were. It wasn't just those cameras, though. He either managed to completely change the way he looked beyond recognition, or he managed to avoid every single camera in the vicinity of the Hatton Garden robbery for two nights running.

He knew the building itself intimately and had keys to many different parts of the building. He seems to have had a key to the look-out post at number 25 too. Perhaps most importantly of all, he knew how to deal with the alarm in a number of complex ways that suggest inside knowledge. Pure intuition, even Basil-calibre intuition, and street smarts, would not have got him through that alarm.

Even so, when not aware that they were being overheard, Danny and Terry have had plenty to say on Basil's shortcomings. As Danny said, 'Carl is walking around in circles the first night. I said, "Carl do something for fuck sake." It's fucking pricks we were with. Basil never done his right job, Tel.'

Terry concurred, 'No, he fucking didn't the cunt, he fucking didn't, cunt.'

Danny went on, 'He got money for old rope there, Terry', and as Terry said, 'He fucking has.'

But as Danny then wryly observed of Basil, 'Never get nicked in a million years, Tel.'

Terry agreed, saying, 'Not a fucking chance on this earth.'

This conversation, captured on police surveillance, has an eerie quality to it now. Perhaps that's because when Danny and Terry were having it they didn't know they were about to get caught themselves, but there does seem to be something fatalistic about it.

We know that Basil left with the rest of the gang in the white van that drove to Bletsoe Walk on the Saturday morning. We know that Basil was back at Bletsoe Walk for the crucial divvy-up on the Monday.

He was still very camera-shy at this point, too. Basil managed to get in and out of Bletsoe Walk without driving past the Cropley Street CCTV camera. To put this feat into perspective, all the other gang members have a starring role on the Cropley Street camera, as you would expect. But not Basil.

Several of the gang members and their associates have indicated to me that the robbery wasn't random. After all, there are plenty of more straightforward places to break into and steal jewels. They imply that Basil went in to get one thing. But they don't know what. And is that even true or is it a red herring for me?

It seems relatively clear that Basil was the only one to take a gold bar. Was that his full and final payment or his equivalent cut to the three holdalls the gang had stashed away? It also seems pretty obvious that Basil had no interest in jewellery.

Danny said to Terry, 'I remember… Tel it was full of fucking bracelets and necklaces, full of them, I said fucking hell.' So, Danny at least was impressed by this aspect of the hoard.

Terry agreed. 'Look to be fair if someone was to throw us those bracelets… you never know. Cos I was thinking I've not even seen the parcel. I'm sitting there with the gold with Basil – all I could hear was him say, "It's shit, throw that away."'

'They are the £500 rings,' Danny noted.

Terry added, 'I said leave off and I did.'

Danny repeated Terry's phrase, then added, 'You know them big wraps about, I don't know, 70, 80 rings on them, I sold the whole lot for fifty grand.'

This is a critical point. This might have seemed like small beans to Basil, not worth the hassle, not thinking big the way Basil liked to think.

We know that Basil was ruthlessly pragmatic too.

As Danny said soon after the robbery to Terry, 'I'll tell you something now, if we never proceeded, me and you, Basil would have walked away.'

'Yeah, he would have,' concurred Terry.

Danny was pondering, looking back on that nightmare first night of the job. 'I'm telling you don't fucking worry about that, if he never see no signs of getting in he ain't going to drill seven or eight holes.'

From intriguing conversations like these, it seems obvious that Danny and Terry were really questioning exactly how much value Basil had added to the job afterwards. Maybe they were questioning the share he had taken of the haul too…

The gold bar plus the cash and foreign currency he took sorted his portion and eliminated any further interest he could take in the loot within the holdalls. But what about his stake in the high-value goods once they got sorted out? Of course, the insurance claim for a further seven million pounds has big implications for Basil too. Put simply, he might have taken a lot more than anyone originally thought, which further explodes the theory that he went in, and went to all that trouble, to put it mildly, for 'just one thing'.

The gang would never talk to any outsider the way they talk about him to each other in the transcripts.

They have also told me that on multiple occasions, the police leaked stories to the press to try and turn them all against one another. This is a strategy that the police, unsurprisingly, wholly deny.

The gang tell me that the police released particular sections of the transcripts where they slag each other off in order to try and break the gang, turn on one another and reveal the locations of the rest of the loot. Of course, whether the police were playing this game or not, this sort of disruptive behaviour combined with the leaks might possibly lead to a slip-up which exploded Basil's hard-won anonymity too.

Divide and rule.

But the gang tell me they were all on to it as a group and kept strong, not rising to it as a tactic. They also tell me that the published photograph of Basil 'leaving' the job (you can't see his face, though) has been completely misunderstood. It isn't him leaving – it is him going in.

After talking to everyone for over a year and thinking about it endlessly, I have come to the conclusion that the robbery was not about one thing. It was about everything. And that because they didn't know quite what they were going to get, their after-plan was poorly thought out, much like the Great

Train Robbers before them. If they knew for instance that they were going to get half a tonne of gold, then they would have lined up a gold man, a smelter and a buyer.

In reality, they smashed open what they could a night later than they hoped. They didn't know what was in the boxes and they ended up with bags and bags of bangles, trinkets, rings, cash. It was baffling and chaotic.

I tried to ask Tom Manson about Basil when I met him in late January 2017. He looked at me searchingly. He didn't disagree with my assertion that Basil was Brian's man and was brought to the job by Brian Reader but he wouldn't confirm it either. He scoffed at the idea that he was an 'inside man'. Not to say that Basil couldn't have had access to the vaults as a contractor or visitor at some stage. In Tom's view hundreds of people would have passed in and out of that place.

Fascination with Basil in particular as well as the case in general has certainly persisted in the press. The familiar themes of Basil being in Panama or an ex-cop were out there, but with no fresh evidence.

Many of the theories circulating in the popular press seemed sensationalised, covering every angle from

Basil being hunted by hitmen attracted by a bounty on his head, sheltered by Russian gangsters, or in permanent hiding from some shadowy fraternity who objected to his level of inside knowledge.

It does seem likely that Basil had some inside knowledge, as I have previously discussed, but that inside knowledge, as my senior police sources made clear to me, could come from an awfully wide range of places. It turns out that Hatton Garden is a surprisingly permeable environment for all its much-trumpeted security and surveillance.

One of the things Jon and Val told me during our meetings was that there is a twist to this story. That there is something funny at the heart of it that nobody knows, that puts a different light on everything. But despite my pushing, they would never reveal what it was.

A casual conversation with Jeff Pope and Terry Winsor in May 2017 led me to think that maybe I had worked out this peculiar twist. What if his name is in fact Baz and their London accents led a police transcriber to write it down as Basil. For instance, say out loud the words 'Baz will never get caught in a million years' or 'Baz will take that one'. It sounds like Basil! And that basic error could be at the root of all the confusion. It certainly isn't the craziest theory out there about Basil.

How much closer anyone is getting to apprehending Basil depends on who you speak to. But they haven't got him. Yet.

EPILOGUE

It's not easy to write an epilogue for a story that is nowhere near done yet. Among the many loose ends for the robbers, the biggest is the 2018 confiscation hearing.

This is where a judge decides once and for all what the gang gained from the raid. If they can't, or won't, pay it back, they could be looking up to an extra 14 years of jail time without parole. That comes on top of their original sentences.

Danny and four of the others were sent down for seven years, and were expecting to be freed in 2019, having served half their sentence plus time on remand before the trial even started. The confiscation hearing could turn all of that on its head.

It's not just Danny, either. The confiscation hearing affects all of them. It's worth recapping on these guys' ages: at the time of writing this book Brian Reader is 78, Terry Perkins is 68, John Collins is 76 and even the baby, Billy the Fish, is 60. Four of the others convicted over the Hatton Garden heist are subject to the confiscation hearing too. The full hearing doesn't even start until 15 January 2018, and it could last about six weeks. There is no guarantee that all the elderly and frail gang members will still be alive even then, let alone at the end of whatever sentences they end up serving.

That's why the new 2017 victim claim that a further £7million was missing and owed to them is so massive. The Prosecutor, Philip Evans, is understandably playing his cards close to his chest on what the new estimate of the final figure on the loot will be. Bet let's just say things aren't looking too rosy for a 2019 release date.

Jeremy Dein had a postscript for me too, one which he was kind enough to come up with during a holiday walk by the sea.

'Does the Hatton Garden robbery suggest that there is a level of criminal mind society just cannot cope with? These guys appear to have had no fear of long sentences despite their ages. The threat of prison seems to have been irrelevant to them – they are career criminals, and we do not seem to have found an answer to offenders like this. I have often represented career criminals without any apparent fear of being locked up – so the whole exercise is no more than a containing exercise. Will offenders like the Hatton Garden robbers ever be rehabilitated? Almost certainly not. If they were physically able, I suspect they would do it all again and die in prison without too many concerns – extraordinary!'

This being the case, Dick Hobbs and Paul Lashmar's closing words (first published in *The Conversation* on 9 March 2016) about the heist are particularly poignant: 'For all that Hatton Garden has sought to clean up its image as a respectable centre for the jewellery trade, serious criminality – lured by the sparkle of gems and the serious money changing hands – is never far away… It's likely that some of the robbery team may die in jail – their older ages have led some to nickname them the "grandpa gang". But the Hatton Garden Heist is a reminder that despite the vast sums of money to be gleaned from the drug trade, from people trafficking and of course from fraud, commercial burglary will never go entirely out of date. As legendary gangster Charles "Lucky" Luciano explained, "Everybody has a little larceny in them," and particularly for professional criminals, the lure of life-changing wealth will always merit serious consideration.'

It has been a hell of a journey, with plenty of hard lessons along the way. I have had my preconceptions, good and bad, about the gang turned on their head. I have learned so much from the police and my network of top lawyers too.

Most of us will never have any idea what goes on behind the scenes in Britain's 21st century world of crime and punishment. Serious and organised crime is getting cleverer and cleverer. It is stronger and more sophisticated than ever before, and it is capable of perpetual metamorphosis.

Have a look at your next-door neighbour, your work colleague, the guy down the gym with a nice watch. Organised criminals today don't hang about on street corners or smoky basements. They are, on the surface, legitimate businessmen and women. And they commit serious criminal acts with a small circle of trusted associates, who are themselves legitimate-seeming and respectable members of society.

Part of the reason why I was so drawn to this case

was because these guys are from the past. They sit in the same pubs they have sat in for 50 years. They look and dress like old cockney villains. As Danny described himself to Martin Brunt, he was just a 'burnt-out burglar', and the others, well 'Dad's Army are like super sportsmen compared with this gang. Run... they can barely walk. One has cancer, he's 70, another heart condition 68. Another 75 can't remember his name. 60-year-old with two new hips and knees.'

On a humid early July afternoon, I went along to the filming of Jeff Pope's drama about Hatton Garden. The first scene I watched was a corker, with acting legend Timothy Spall as Terry Perkins taking a piss and having a funny turn thanks to his diabetes. Then we went up to the rooftop and shot a group scene with all of them in their blue overalls. The Danny Jones character even had his Montana top on! There was a brilliant atmosphere on set and a sense that something very special was being made out of this amazing story. It was going to be a great series!

On a poignant note, legendary Scotti's Snack Bar on Clerkenwell Green, the meeting place of the robbers on so many occasions, closed its doors forever in 2017. Another piece of history and a window into authentic old London has been lost for ever. A poster outside at the time read 'Keep your head up by aiming for the stars'. We will never see a British job quite like the Hatton Garden heist again.

HATTON GARDEN HEIST AND BEYOND: THE BASIC TIMELINE

Mid-February–late March 2015 The gang met a number of times and carried out reconnaissance around the Hatton Garden Safe Deposit Company vault.

2–4 April 2015 The gang assembled and then the burglary took place over two separate nights across the bank holiday weekend.

5–6 April 2015 The gang dispersed and began the complex process of hiding and distributing the loot.

7 April 2015 The audacious raid was discovered by the security guards arriving back at the Hatton Garden Safe Deposit after the long weekend

April–mid-May 2015 Unbeknown to the gang, the police surveillance had started in earnest. From 14 May onwards, the investigators also bugged Terry and Kenny's vehicles. Plenty of incriminating material was captured on video and audio in the process and subsequently used to establish the case for the prosecution.

19 May 2015 Police raid at Sterling Road where loot was seized and the men were arrested. Further arrests of other suspected gang members took place later that same day.

4 September 2015 The culmination of the court case against the gang. Danny, Terry, Kenny and Brian all pleaded guilty to conspiracy to commit burglary. During the trial, showman Danny promised the police that he would happily lead them to his stash.

8 October 2015 The police conducted a fruitful search of an Edmonton graveyard, where they turned up two bags stuffed with expensive jewels under the tombstones of various members of Val's family.

15 October 2015 Danny took a little trip out of Belmarsh prison under police escort. The purpose of the trip was for him to take the officers to the place, or places, where had said he had hidden the stolen goods.

23 November 2015 The trial of Carl Wood, Jon Harbinson, Billy Lincoln and Hugh Doyle began at Woolwich Crown Court. Jon was cleared of the two offences after saying he had no idea what was inside the bags that were put in his taxi.

March 2016 Sentencing at Woolwich Crown Court. Danny Jones, Terry Perkins and Kenny Collins were all jailed for seven years for conspiracy to commit burglary. Carl Wood and Billy Lincoln were given six and seven years respectively, for the same offence and one count of and conspiracy to conceal, convert or transfer criminal property, after a trial. Brian Reader, was too ill to attend court after suffering a second stroke and was only sentenced later on. Hugh Doyle received a suspended sentence after he was found guilty of concealing, converting or transferring criminal property between 1 January and 19 May last year.

6 January 2017 The Metropolitan Police confirmed that they were investigating claims an extra £7 million in gold was stolen during the Hatton Garden raid. A woman came forward claiming she only realised her safety deposit box was missing after the trial of the gang who carried out the raid. It could mean the total stolen in the burglary stands at around £21 million. Scotland Yard issued a statement confirming that her claim was received in June 2016.

31 January 2017 Another development in the POCA saga. The value of the goods stolen in the Hatton Garden jewellery raid had risen to an estimated £25 million. It was originally thought the value of the items stolen over the 2015 Easter holiday was £14 million. But Woolwich Crown Court heard that prosecutors are now seeking the larger sum from the five men convicted of the robbery. If they do not pay back the sum they face a maximum of 14 years being added to their sentences without parole. The court heard that the full confiscation hearing is expected to last around six weeks.

January 2018 The full confiscation hearing is scheduled to begin, although of course this date may be subject to further change. Whenever it does eventually take place, it will be the next big milestone in the long and painful legal process swirling around this incredible ongoing saga.